LOST AND FOUND

The dank basement of the Golub home was filled with a nearly unbelievable amount of clutter and trash. Much of it appeared to have been simply tossed down the stairs. The police had to push aside broken glass, litter, folded carpet remnants, boxes and piles of newspapers as they walked across the room in search of clues to the disappearance of thirteen-year-old Kelly Ann Tinyes.

Beneath the stairway was a small closet with a closed door, blocked by a steamer trunk piled high with other items.

"What's in here?" Officer Charney asked John Golub, Sr.

"That's a storage area."

Both men moved the trunk and opened the door a short distance. Peering inside the closet with his flashlight, Charney noticed a greenish zippered sleeping bag inclined awkwardly against the wall. He crawled into the dark space, caught the zipper and pulled it down a few inches. The light fell on what appeared to be a female leg covered with dried blood.

He called to Detective McVetty across the room. McVetty crawled into the closet and knelt down. At first, he thought the leg he saw might belong to a large doll or model form, so he pressed a single finger gently against the surface. As soon as he touched the skin, he knew.

This was human flesh.

AGAINST HER WILL

RONALD J. WATKINS

PINNACLE BOOKS
KENSINGTON PUBLISHING CORP.
http://www.kensingtonbooks.com

Please note that some names have been changed to protect the privacy of some individuals mentioned in this book.

PINNACLE BOOKS are published by

Kensington Publishing Corp.
850 Third Avenue
New York, NY 10022

Copyright © 1995 by Ronald J. Watkins

The P logo Reg. U.S. Pat. & TM Off. Pinnacle is a trademark of Kensington Publishing Corp.

First Printing: June, 1995

10 9 8 7 6 5

Printed in the United States of America

FOR JO ANN

Acknowledgments

I must thank my agent, Mike Hamilburg, for bringing this project to my attention, and Charles "Butch" Fries who brought it to him. Thanks as always to Joanie Socola for her assistance and patience.

I also thank Paul Dinas, who took a chance on the story when others had passed. Thanks to him for his suggestions, editing, and support. Thanks as well to Debbie Cohen, editorial assistant at Pinnacle, for her help.

My two daughters, Theresa and Elizabeth, were a tremendous assistance to me as well. Theresa transcribed many of the interviews that are the core of this book. She was also fired from her job when I was researching my last book simply for being my daughter. It was an insensitive act that caused her much pain and I neglected to publicly express my sympathy the last time out. Elizabeth checked details from research material and was responsible for placing the witnesses at the trial in proper sequence since my research material had them jumbled. For this, for their love and support, I thank them both.

My thanks to Richard Wells, John Nolan, Lorah McNally, Roberta Grosse, Salvatore Marinello, and many others for their time and assistance.

Thanks also to Dr. Hector V. Gonzalez for deciphering the complex odontology testimony.

John and Elizabeth Golub were approached in person and by letter to request their assistance and they refused. I exchanged letters with Robert Golub who declined to be interviewed unless he was paid, something I would not do. I met with Richard and Victoria Tinyes for about an hour. They also demanded payment for cooperation, payment I declined to make.

Finally, my deepest appreciation and thanks to my wife, Jo Ann, for transcribing the trial and my many hours of taped interviews, for her review of source material, her comments, suggestions, proofing of the manuscript, and unswerving support.

O, what may man within him hide,
Though angel on the outward side!
                                        —William Shakespeare

Preface

Why write about murder?

It is a question I have never been asked, yet it is one I have posed to myself a thousand times. I confess to a certain ambivalence each time I approach another project that will end in a book such as this. When asked by friends or curious strangers what I am writing now, I am more often apologetic than prideful as I describe the project. There is so much violence in the media, so much death, misery and mayhem that are exploited by the tabloids, I struggle with each book to be certain I am not simply producing one more piece of sordid journalism, meant only to appeal to prurient pleasures.

The readers of my books and of this genre, however, never express such reservations to me. Indeed, they cannot get enough. Consumers of true crime are among the most voracious and loyal of readers. Life is filled with ambiguity and uncertainty and I suspect this keen interest stems from the understanding that with death there are no second chances, no opportunities to make amends, no means to change its certainty. Because of that finality and the surety that it comes to everyone, death holds a special fascination for us.

In nearly every situation murder is a sordid business. Drunken, foolish people slay one another and are often caught at the crime scene. Family members kill one another and are immediately remorseful. Such is murder as it is seen by police officers every day. But sometimes the manner of a death stands out so starkly that we must gaze at it unavoidably, unable to turn our attention elsewhere, enraptured and horrified simultaneously.

The taking of human life and the manner of that taking says a great deal about a single individual; in some instances it says far more about what we are as people, about the depth of our capacities. For in murder, both victim and killer are human and it is that realization as well that holds us transfixed in its presence.

There is an aspect of this fascination that is troubling. The truth is that crime has not increased in America for the last twenty years relative to population, but our concern over it has. We feel less secure than ever in our homes and neighborhoods. There have always been killers among us, but now, with a media focused so heavily on them, we see and hear about every murder of consequence in the nation. Little wonder that we think murderers are running amok.

Still we do have the need to know, to attempt an understanding. It seems to me that much of this interest in killing demonstrates that murder is so far removed from normal life that it represents an aberration. We want to comprehend, and it is in that human response we find the answer to the question: Why write about murder? I write about it because only humankind commits murder. All other creatures kill to eat, kill to survive, kill their young so the strong can live. Only we kill out of malice, in rage—or for the shear pleasure of the act.

In comprehending the enormity of murder, in grappling with its devious motives, we are reassured of our own fundamental decency. To the extent we comprehend murder, so do we understand ourselves.

This book, and others like it, are also forewarnings, cautionary tales, told to alert us all to greater vigilance. For among us are predators who live by day as normal men, but in the blackness of night and in the crawl spaces of their dwellings, exist as men driven by forces virtually beyond our comprehension, taking pleasure from inflicting terror and consuming innocent life.

And they are always someone's son, another's brother, and everyone's neighbor.

Ronald J. Watkins
Rua Luciano Cordeiro
Lisbon, Portugal

Prologue

The mother had put on her jacket against the cold of the night. She had been up this street a thousand times before in the many years she had lived here, but never like this.

Where could my daughter be? she asked herself. She has never done anything like this before.

Ever since arriving home that Friday afternoon from work the mother had done nothing but search for her thirteen-year-old, her oldest child, her only daughter—her baby. She and her husband had telephoned neighbors, family friends, friends of her daughter, then called them again and again.

She was so reliable, so responsible, how could this happen? She had told her younger brother she was going to visit a girlfriend up the street, but the girl said she had never arrived.

Where could she be?

This was their street, their neighborhood. The mother knew every member of every family on the street by name and by sight. What could possibly have happened? If her daughter wasn't safe here, where could she possibly be safe?

Why had she left the house when she had been told

to stay? Why had she said she was going to her friend's, and then not arrived?

Where could she be?

Verging on hysterics, the mother knocked on doors she had been to previously but again found no answers.

Back on the sidewalk she pulled her jacket tightly about her. *My God. Where could she be?*

One

Middle America is spread across the nation. It can be in Kansas, Oregon, Alabama, and even in New York. Middle America is a way of living, with blocks of homes, children playing in yards, or stickball in the streets. It is neighborhood schools and churches. It is fathers leaving for work in the morning, returning at night, tired, but taking the time to listen to their children, to discipline them as necessary, to comfort them when needed. It is mothers taking care of the house, handling most of the child rearing, but increasingly, mothers also going off to work only to work again when they come home.

There are many such places around New York City. One of them is a large suburban area called Long Island, which lies to the south and east of Manhattan. Shaped like a fish, it runs 130 miles from its "head" in Brooklyn to its "tail" in Montauk Point and thirty miles across at its midsection.

Settled first in a series of hamlets, thickly wooded Long Island became the first vast stretch of American suburbia and despite a declining population remains a largely affluent series of interlocking bedroom communities for Manhattan.

One of these towns is Valley Stream, as typical as any on Long Island, as sleepy and middle-American as its name suggests. Murder here is virtually nonexistent. Before 1989 the last had taken place in a nearby community when a sixteen-year-old boy had been stabbed to death by a deranged man. That had been in 1977.

Nineteen families live on Horton Road in Valley Stream, five of them have been in residence since 1936. The neighborhood is divided almost in half into two styles of well-maintained homes. The first is composed of small Cape Cod-style houses and driving from the south toward the first house to the right is that of the Tinyes family. Four houses down their side of the street begin taller white stucco and red brick Tudor-style homes, the first of which, in the middle of the block, is that of the Golub family.

Most of the families on Horton Road have children and they serve as a bond for the adults. The children attend Woodmere Middle School or Hewlett High School and the neighborhood is largely Catholic. Not far away is Grant Park ice rink and near it is Carolla's pizza parlor.

Those living on Horton Road are by most standards quite comfortable. There is an electrician living there, a typesetter, owners of small businesses, along with a scattering of professionals who take the Long Island Railroad and commute into Manhattan each day.

The families on Horton Road also share a sense of community. Several years ago the parents banded together and petitioned the city to have the street converted one-way to cut down on traffic. On Halloween, Labor Day, and the Fourth of July, the parents hold a block party to keep the children close and from harm's way.

This is suburbia, as American, as tranquil, as any

neighborhood in Des Moines, Iowa, Culver City, California, or Tyler, Texas. It is a quiet neighborhood and there is an unspoken covenant shared by all on Horton Road just as there is in all of suburbia: Neighbors tend to the outward appearance of their houses, and they watch out for one another's children. And until 1989, everyone on Horton Road lived by it.

Friday, March 3, 1989, was a clear day near winter's end, and it would be the last day of peace for Horton Road, the end of a tranquility that had begun with the construction of the houses before the Second World War. This day would be a demarcation, as final as any catastrophe and just as permanent in the minds of those who live there. For the rest of their lives they would know what they had been doing, where they were, when thirteen-year-old Kelly Ann Tinyes entered the house of her neighbor at 81 Horton Road.

After school that day Richard Tinyes had driven his daughter, Kelly, home as was often his custom. En route she asked if she could go ice-skating at Grant Park, but instead her father told her to baby-sit her eight-year-old brother Richie until her mother came home from work.

Kelly was the oldest of the two Tinyes children. Her house had been the home of her father's parents who were now invalid and lived there still. The Tinyes family had moved into the red-painted house with white shutters and trim in 1967. They were quiet, well-regarded neighbors who waved as they drove down the street on their way to work.

Kelly's father, Richard, age thirty-six, was a tall, burly man with a beard and dark blond hair. He operated Victoria's Auto Repairs, hardly more than a stall not far from home where he restored cars to support his family. Her mother, Victoria, was thirty-four years old that day, a quiet, strong-willed woman and the dominant voice in the family. She worked at a local doctor's office. That afternoon Kelly's grandfather was in the hospital dying of cancer, her grandmother upstairs in her sickbed.

Because of her grandparents' declining health Kelly spent more time alone at home with them than was typical for girls her age, playing with her dog, Brutus. She rarely had friends over to visit, spending time in their homes instead. The Tinyes's house was not large and it was not easy with so many under one roof. But Kelly never talked about it to her friends. She performed her duty with her grandparents as necessary.

Kelly was tall for her age at five feet eight inches and weighed 120 pounds. She wore her long brown hair down her back, often held on top of her head with a clip. She had a habit of tossing it with the movement of her head in a manner that became her trademark. She had a warm, generous smile, and outgoing disposition.

So deep was the blue of her eyes that the year before when she and her four closest friends assigned one another nicknames, Kelly had been named Sky.

She was a responsible, levelheaded daughter, reliable and conscientious. She was neat and organized far beyond her years, even maintaining a calendar of her activities. More than anything she loved to ice-skate and did so at every opportunity, so it was a disappointment when her father told her she must baby-sit her younger brother.

Most of the children on Horton Road were younger

than Kelly yet she often played games with them. She would be mother or their older sister or the lady who came to buy goods at their make-believe stores. She had a friend her own age, Sharon Stonel, five doors down on the other side of the street and she went there often to visit.

Every street has gregarious neighbors known to all. Every street has quiet families who keep to themselves and avoid contact. Such were the Golubs.

The father, John, age fifty-seven, was very short, not many inches over five feet and walked with a decided limp from a childhood bout with polio. He was a taciturn man, even glum, but a hard worker. He operated a Getty service station not far away in Hewlett and repaired cars in its bin. He spent much of his free time with his boat or tinkering with a Rolls-Royce he was restoring.

His wife, Elizabeth, was forty-eight years old, heavyset and even shorter than her husband. She had been active in the petition drive to convert the street to one-way and as a consequence had several close friends among their neighbors. She regularly attended a Tuesday night prayer group at St. Joseph's Roman Catholic Church and each of her children had been confirmed there. She worked at a local transportation company office and routinely shopped at garage and tag sales.

The couple had three children. Their first was a daughter, Adele, who lived in Manhattan, had graduated from college, and worked at an accounting firm. She was engaged and would be marrying soon. When Elizabeth had been pregnant with her next child they moved onto Horton Road, by coincidence the same year as the Tinyes family. Not long after the move she gave birth to a boy, now twenty-one years old, named Robert. Her final child was also a son, fourteen-year-old John, always called John Jay to distinguish him from his father.

Roberta Grosse was Kelly's best friend and had been since nursery school. The two often walked home together since Kelly's house was on the way. The following Sunday, March 5, was Kelly's fourteenth birthday. The girls did not date, but the last year had been a busy one for them and their friends. Woodmere Middle School with six hundred students was about sixty percent Jewish and regardless of their faith the girls attended a Bar or Bat Mitzvah nearly every weekend. They went to movies together, ice-skated, hung out, and talked about boys.

For weeks the group of four girls with whom Kelly was closest had debated what to buy for her birthday. The girls agreed on a pair of amethyst earrings which Roberta had carefully wrapped and placed in her bedroom dresser. Roberta suggested they take Kelly to dinner that night, then have her stay overnight when the other girls would join them in a surprise slumber party. Plans were made and Kelly's mother had agreed.

It was customary for Roberta and Kelly to talk on the telephone after school. Roberta worked at a travel agency and recently her boss had complained about her tying up the business line with her personal calls. So on this day she waited a bit for an opportunity before making her call.

After she arrived home Kelly called her friend Jennifer, but no one answered. Kelly called her father at work and once again he told her that she could not go ice-skating, but must stay home with her brother for another hour until her mother arrived from work. "Ask your mother then. You know she'll let you go. She always does."

Kelly called another girlfriend to learn why she had not attended school that day, then complained to her that she was being forced to baby-sit her brother. She said she was thinking about just leaving the house anyway and going to Grant Park.

Just after the conversation ended Richie answered the telephone. The caller said his name was John and he asked to speak to Kelly. His sister took the call and spoke briefly. About twenty minutes later, at 3:10 P.M. Kelly told her brother that she was going to Nichol's house just down the street and would be right back.

Richie waited only five minutes for his sister to return. It was not like her to leave him alone when she was supposed to be sitting so he decided to find his sister. At about 3:15 he walked down the sidewalk to thirteen-year-old Nichol's house, but she told him Kelly had not been there. Six-year-old Harry Finny, for whom Kelly had often sat, was playing in front of Sharon Stonel's house, which was between Nichol's and the Golubs' homes. When Richie told him he was looking for his sister, Harry told him that he had just seen Kelly go into John Jay's house. The children walked to the front door and standing on the Golubs' porch rang the doorbell repeatedly. No one answered.

Back at his house by 3:45 P.M. Richie called both his mother and father, who worked nearby, to tell them that Kelly had left him alone and not returned. His mother, Victoria, said she would be home within the hour. When Richie mentioned the Golubs' home to his father, he said, "Go find Kelly, Richie. Go to the Golub house and beat on the door and call out for your sister."

The Tinyes and Golub families scarcely knew each other. There was no reason for Kelly to be there. It was not that Richard was alarmed so much as this was out of the ordinary. If Kelly was there her brother was to get her back home.

But first Richie found the number for the Golubs and called several times without an answer. Then Richie walked up the street to do as he was told. He pounded the door with his fists, calling out for Kelly, over and over. From inside pulsated heavy rock music that drowned out the eight-year-old's every sound.

Richie went back to the sidewalk and there called out for his sister. "Kelly! Brutus is loose. Get out here quick. Kelly!" The eight-year-old had reasoned that if his sister believed her dog was out of the house she would be more likely to come right away. Richie walked up and down Horton Road calling out over and over, his child's voice echoing along the street, but no one came.

Back at the house Richie answered the telephone hoping to hear his sister's voice, but instead it was Roberta asking to talk to Kelly. Roberta was puzzled that Kelly would have been gone so long. She and Kelly had intended to talk on the telephone and make further plans for that night. Two more times during the next hour Roberta called, growing increasingly concerned.

Victoria arrived just after five P.M. followed shortly thereafter by her husband. The couple was upset that their reliable oldest daughter was still missing and telephoned a series of her friends without success.

By now Roberta was home from work and the second

time Richard called to ask for his daughter he was quite accusatory. "If Kelly is there you better tell me," he told her. But all Roberta could say was that she was as puzzled as Mr. Tinyes.

Both parents continued calling every friend of their daughter's they could think of, speaking to some more than once, but no one had heard from Kelly, except Jennifer and Kelly's other friend, and no one claimed to know where she was. Gradually apprehension overwhelmed anger.

Victoria walked up and down Horton Road, knocking on the doors of neighbors and friends, but no one knew where her daughter was. Finally she spoke to Sharon Stonel who said she had seen Kelly enter the Golubs' house shortly after three o'clock. This reinforced what Richie had told Victoria, but it struck the mother as odd now just as it had when he had first mentioned it. While it was true that the Golubs had a fourteen-year-old son, John Jay, who Kelly knew casually from the neighborhood, the pair were not friends, at least not to her mother's knowledge.

Five times between 4:53 P.M. and 5:30 P.M. someone from the Tinyes household had attempted to reach someone at the Golubs' house by telephone without success. Just before six o'clock Richard called the Golubs' residence still again and spoke to Elizabeth, who told him that Kelly had not been to her house. It had taken a moment for Elizabeth to remember just who the girl was since the Golubs and Tinyes were not close. Richard asked to speak directly with John Jay and Elizabeth put him on the telephone.

"Did you see Kelly earlier today?" Richard asked.

John Jay said that he had not, that he last saw Kelly several days ago.

It seemed to Richard that the boy was very nervous. "Are you sure?" he asked.

"Yeah," the fourteen-year-old mumbled, seemingly eager to get off the telephone.

Roberta called for her friend through the early evening hours, but the Tinyes telephone was busy until just after six P.M. Before she could inquire if Kelly was home, Richard Tinyes asked, "Do you know where she is?" Roberta did not and she thought she could detect fear in the man's voice.

Roberta, Kelly, and their three other girlfriends were all to have gathered at the Grosses' house at eight o'clock and walk to dinner at a nearby Chinese restaurant from there. The girlfriends came over even though no one had heard from Kelly. A sense of foreboding settled onto the evening's plans, and the girls spoke among themselves in endless and ultimately circular conversation speculating about what could have happened.

Kelly's parents sounded increasingly frantic in their repeated calls to each of them. In a somber mood the girls went to the nearby restaurant to eat but the evening was nothing like they had intended. As they were walking back to the Grosses' house, Kelly's parents drove up and asked the girls still again if any of them knew anything about their daughter. Back at Roberta's by ten o'clock it was apparent there would be no slumber party and one by one the girls returned home. Roberta began crying.

Richard and Victoria continued making calls and knocking on doors until it was very late. By now they were a jumble of contrary emotions. Anger, apprehension, frustration, and nagging fear were mixed together, aggravated by fatigue. They drove around the neighborhood searching, then went to Roberta's house to demand she tell them where Kelly was. "Don't lie to us," Richard said. But Roberta knew nothing.

As the Tinyes drove off Roberta was in hysterics. She could see the fear in their eyes, the desperation in their demands. When Roberta finally did go to bed after midnight, she insisted her parents awaken her if they heard anything about Kelly, and she made her father, who liked Kelly very much, promise that no matter where she was he would drive and pick her up if for some reason she was afraid to call home.

At about three A.M. the telephone rang at the Grosse's home and Roberta's father answered it. Roberta was by his side immediately. It was Linda Player, Kelly's favorite aunt, asking still again if the Grosse's knew anything at all about Kelly. Roberta, thinking it was Kelly on the telephone said, "Wherever she is, go get her, Dad."

Linda Player asked to talk to Roberta and again wanted to know if the teenager knew where Kelly was. She did not.

Lying in bed after the call Roberta's worst nightmare asserted itself repeatedly. In her fear and anguish she imagined that Kelly had been abducted and murdered. No, she told herself, that couldn't have happened, not to Kelly. But over and over the vision pressed itself into her thoughts and when at last Roberta did sleep the nightmare remained, so powerful, so real it was as if it had already taken place.

* * *

Shortly before midnight the telephone rang at the Golubs' home, awakening Elizabeth from sleep. "Do you know what time it is?" she asked the caller, irritated at the late-hour interruption. The unidentified caller was assisting the Tinyes family and explained that Kelly from down the street had been missing since that afternoon. Neighbor children claimed to have seen her enter the Golub house. The caller asked Elizabeth to awaken John Jay and find out if he had talked to Kelly earlier that day.

Elizabeth went down the hall to her youngest son's bedroom. A sleepy-eyed John Jay denied seeing Kelly. Elizabeth relayed the information and said that she hoped they found the girl.

Elizabeth was no longer irritated. What parent could fail to sympathize with what was happening to the Tinyes family? Before going back to bed Elizabeth went down the stairs to her front door and opened it. The cold night air poured into the warm house and she stood there in her robe staring at the Tinyeses' house just five doors away on the same side of the street. She saw no commotion, no police. The street was quiet, with no sign of trouble. She stared a moment longer, then closed the door and went back to her bed.

Inside, the Tinyeses' house was near panic. Victoria's sister, Linda Player, and her husband had been there most of the night to assist in the search. Sharing his daughter's concern, Roberta's father made several calls that night but found the Tinyeses' telephone constantly busy. Far into the morning hours the group at the Tinyeses' house called everyone they could think of.

What could have happened? they asked themselves repeatedly. It seemed impossible that Kelly would run away, but maybe she had. God forbid, what if a stranger had picked her up and carried her off? Why hadn't she gone to see her girlfriend like she said, and why did her girlfriend insist she had gone into the Golubs' house when the family said she hadn't? There were questions, endless questions, and no answers during that long, frantic night.

At 1:40 A.M. Richard called the police and was told they must wait until morning before they could help. By four A.M. the exhausted couple nodded off for a fitful, short-lived sleep.

Two

The Tinyeses were up early on Saturday, exhausted from the previous night, upset, fearful, and agitated. Immediately they retraced their steps. Richard went down the street with his sister-in-law Linda and knocked on the Golubs' door. He told Elizabeth that Kelly had not come home over night and they were desperate to locate her.

"I can't believe it," Elizabeth replied. She told him about the call she had received during the night. Richard asked if she would speak to her son again. They were rechecking every detail possible and so far the only lead they had was the Stonel girl who said she had seen Kelly go into the Golubs' house. Elizabeth let the couple into her foyer, then went upstairs to talk to her son again.

Neither Richard nor Linda had ever been inside the Golubs' home previously. Standing just inside the door they expressed surprise to one another at the condition of the house. While the exterior of the Golubs' home was consistently neat and well-maintained, indeed Elizabeth was often seen by neighbors sweeping her driveway in her heels, the inside was so cluttered it was difficult to make out the living-room furniture.

Upstairs John Jay was still sleeping. When his mother

awakened him he told her that he had not seen or spoken to Kelly the day before. Elizabeth went back down the stairs and relayed the information. Richard asked her to let her neighbors know Kelly was missing. Back at his house, running out of alternatives, Richard called the police once again.

Detective Thomas McVetty of the Juvenile Aid Bureau, Fifth Precinct, Nasssu County Police Department, had come on duty that Saturday morning and as was customary checked the computer screen for new cases. At once he spotted the missing persons report filed earlier by Richard Tinyes. He called the Tinyeses' home and reached Linda Player. From Kelly's aunt he obtained a description, general background on the missing girl, Linda's thoughts as to where she might be, and the telephone numbers of friends.

McVetty spoke to one to see if Kelly was having any trouble her parents might not know about and learned of none. Kelly did not sound like the kind of girl to suddenly turn up missing. Then a few minutes later Linda called and asked him to come to the Tinyeses' home. McVetty responded with another juvenile officer, Detective Brennen, a former nun turned police officer.

At 10:20 that morning the pair met with Richard and Victoria Tinyes at their home. They told the officers that Kelly was of good mental and physical health, that something such as this was highly unusual. Kelly did not drink alcohol, did not use drugs, did not smoke, and was not promiscuous. She had no boyfriend.

McVetty commented that fourteen-year-olds do things

like this sometimes and that they shouldn't be too concerned.

"Not Kelly," her mother said fiercely. "Kelly doesn't do this."

The parents also told McVetty that Sharon Stonel was reporting that she had seen Kelly enter the Golubs' home the previous afternoon. The Golubs insisted she had never gone into the house, but no one in the neighborhood reported seeing their daughter after that. The trail led to the Golubs' house and stopped. The families hardly knew each other and Kelly had no business they could think of with any member of the Golub household. Until today when Richard and his sister-in-law had gone down the street to talk to Mrs. Golub, no one in the Tinyes family had ever been inside the Golubs' house. They didn't know what to make of it.

Following the interview McVetty and Brennen walked up the street toward the Golubs' house. At this point all the police had was a missing persons report, and a missing young teenager was not that extraordinary. It was something they saw nearly every working day. Usually there was very little behind it and the teenager turned up within hours. Even the twenty-odd hours Kelly had been missing was not that unusual, especially since it included overnight. Teenage girls might stay with a friend, spend a night with a boyfriend, or run away from home. No matter how normal the family appeared, how decent the people involved, such occurrences could happen in any family.

Still this was different. It wasn't likely the girl would disappear on her best friends when they were planning a slumber party, or be missing the day before her birthday.

* * *

After Richard Tinyes and Linda Player left her house earlier, Elizabeth Golub had gone to the nearby King Kullen market to shop, and on the way back stopped at several houses to ask if anyone knew anything about the missing Tinyes girl. She went last to the Tinyeses' house to see if their daughter had returned. Victoria told her that Sharon Stonel claimed she had seen Kelly enter the Golubs' house.

Back home Elizabeth confronted her son. "John Jay, the Stonel girl said that she saw Kelly enter our house." She demanded an honest answer. Her son replied it wasn't true, then suggested, "Let's go straighten this out." Mother and son walked across the street.

At the Stonel house the girl's father confirmed that his daughter said she had seen Kelly enter the Golubs' house. She was quite certain. Elizabeth wanted to speak to the girl herself and questioned her, asking who had opened the door. Sharon said she couldn't see, but she had watched Kelly go inside. While they were speaking Elizabeth spotted two police officers coming up the walk to her house and went outside to join them.

McVetty and Brennen saw Elizabeth and John Jay approaching them and waited on the porch.

"Are you looking for us?" Elizabeth asked.

"I'm looking for Mrs. Golub," McVetty replied.

"I'm Mrs. Golub. This is my son John Jay."

"We're investigating a missing person, the whereabouts of Kelly Tinyes." McVetty explained that this was the first house at which he had stopped and Elizabeth related what she had been told across the street at the Stonels'.

"Could we do this interview inside?" McVetty asked politely. It was standard police procedure to enter a residence if at all possible when conducting an investigation. Elizabeth invited the officers inside.

Standing in the foyer near the stairs leading to the second story, McVetty asked John Jay if he knew Kelly and if he had seen her the previous day. John Jay said that he did know Kelly and no, he had not seen her. McVetty asked if he knew her whereabouts and again John Jay said he did not.

McVetty asked, "Is anyone else in the house who might know something about Kelly's whereabouts?"

"My brother's in the house," John Jay said. McVetty asked the boy to get his brother so he could speak to him. A few minutes later Robert came down the stairs accompanied by Paul Zerrella, a friend. The chairs in the living room were each covered with piles of clothing and there was nowhere to sit. Without apology Robert took a seat on the lower stairs beside where John Jay was standing while McVetty questioned him.

The contrast between the two brothers was striking. John Jay was a handsome young teenager, of average height with carefully coiffed hair. Kelly had once remarked to a girlfriend that she thought him "cute." Robert was barely more than five feet tall and was powerfully built from weight lifting. It was difficult to imagine the two as brothers.

McVetty spoke to Robert for about five minutes, asking if he knew where Kelly might be and if he had seen her the previous day. Robert said he knew Kelly only by sight, had not seen her for several weeks, and knew nothing about where she might be. McVetty asked where Robert had been on Friday and he said that he had been home all day, from seven in the morning until nine o'clock that night. In response to questions he denied making any telephone calls and he denied having any relationship of any kind with the missing girl.

Zerella interjected that the two of them had been together the previous night and Robert shook his head. "That was later on."

Robert explained that John Jay had two friends over to the house on Friday afternoon and that they had played Nintendo. McVetty noticed that each time Robert answered a question he looked at John Jay for confirmation. The older brother also appeared very nervous to him.

"Why do you keep looking at your brother?" McVetty asked. "Why not just answer the questions straight, without help?"

Robert said, "I'm not sure." He was just trying to help. McVetty took John Jay aside a few feet away and spoke to him further in the living room to receive independent corroboration of what Robert was telling him. John Jay nodded his head to each question. Then the officers thanked the Golubs and crossed the street.

At the Stonels' house Sharon told the detectives that she had seen Kelly enter the Golubs' home the day before at about 3:15. Sharon's mother, Carol, told them that while she had not seen Kelly actually enter the residence she had watched her walking up the street from her house at about this same time. She also told the officers that a neighborhood boy, Harry Finny, just told her he had also seen Kelly enter the Golubs' house and that John Jay had let her in.

This was new information. McVetty and Brennen went down the street to speak to the Finny boy and obtain his statement. He was emphatic about what he had seen. Kelly had gone into the house and John Jay had opened the door for her. The detectives returned to the Stonels' to use the telephone and call a superior.

McVetty explained everything he had learned that morning. Then he said he needed uniformed backup. "I'm going to conduct a search of the Golubs' house," he explained. "I believe that's where this investigation is."

At 11:45 A.M. McVetty and Brennen, accompanied by uniformed officer Howard Charney, who had been summoned to assist, knocked on the Golubs' door. When Elizabeth answered McVetty explained the situation and requested permission to search the Golubs' house. Customarily a search could only be conducted with a court-issued warrant. But it was often the ease in juvenile investigations that parents are more than eager to cooperate and would consent to searches if it would be of help. It was not that uncommon for a runaway to be hiding in someone's bedroom unknown to the parents. For such situations officers carried special forms. McVetty held out a consent authorization he wanted her to sign.

Elizabeth asked the officers into her house, took the paper from McVetty's hand, and stood there staring at the document. McVetty explained to her that he was not looking for drugs and that he would not be searching her dresser drawers or lingerie. He said that he was looking for a living human being who was last seen coming into her house. He wasn't saying she was lying, he wasn't saying she knew the girl was there, but she could be hidden there. This happens all the time in his job.

Elizabeth considered what the officer had to say then responded that of course the officers were free to search. She would do anything she could to assist. Her husband was at the dock working on his boat. It wasn't far away. "Can I wait for my husband?" she asked.

"Go ahead, Mom. Sign it," John Jay urged, but Elizabeth told the officers she would really rather wait for her husband. They agreed.

John Golub belonged to the Keystone Yacht Club and maintained his boat in nearby Woodmere. When his wife explained by telephone what was taking place, he drove home, spoke briefly to the officers, then signed the release without hesitation along with his wife. McVetty suggested Elizabeth accompany Brennen while she searched upstairs, then John Golub, himself, and Charney would start in the basement.

The dank basement was filled with a nearly unbelievable amount of clutter and trash. Much of it appeared to have been simply tossed down the stairs and in only one or two places was it even possible to see the carpeting on the floor. There was no pathway and virtually no room in which to move. The officers had to push items aside to look around with their flashlights. There was broken glass on the floor, litter, folded pieces of carpeting, boxes, piles of newspapers.

McVetty moved carefully across the room to search. Charney looked along the walls and then worked slowly back toward the stairs. The officers moved cautiously and in silence. Beneath the stairway was a small closet with a closed door, blocked by a steamer trunk. Beside it was another bedroom-sized room. In another area was a sink and toilet. Charney spotted the antique steamer trunk in front of the closet with other items lying on it and against the door as well.

"What's in here?" he asked John Golub.

"That's a storage area."

Charney asked Golub to help him and the pair dragged the heavy trunk away. Charney opened the door a short distance. He peered into the dark closet with his flashlight and noticed at once a green zippered sleeping bag that lay half inclined against the wall in an awkward position. Charney crawled into the closet, extended his hand and pressed his fingertips against the sleeping bag. The zipper was toward him and he moved it down a few inches. The cloth separated and his light fell on what appeared to be a human leg, covered with dried blood. He was so startled he gasped and jerked back suddenly.

Once he was composed Charney called to McVetty across the room, "Look at this." John Golub, who had been searching on the other side of the room by now, hurried over as Charney backed up to make room for McVetty.

"What's that? Is it a body?" John asked, then seeing Charney's expression required no answer.

McVetty knelt down, leaned forward, and crawled into the closet. Once he was in position he was startled by what it appeared he was seeing. Then he thought for an instant that what he was looking at through the slot of the open zipper might be a doll so McVetty pressed a single finger gently against the surface, and there was no doubt.

This was human flesh.

Three

McVetty turned to tell John to stay put, that the basement was now a crime scene, but already the man had hurried up the stairs to inform his wife what had just been discovered in their basement. McVetty's concern was now to seal the location until homicide detectives arrived.

"Stay down here and guard this area," he told Charney. The officer nodded his head and as McVetty moved toward the stairs, Charney looked about him with even greater scrutiny. He could see a slip of white paper nearby that looked as if dried blood might be on it. His eyes continued scanning the scene and he spotted other places that might have blood.

By now Brennen had arrived from upstairs. She looked over Charney's shoulder, saw the bloody leg, and nearly gagged. McVetty told her to go to the car and request homicide assistance.

Word seemed to spread from the Golubs' house along Horton Road on its own wings. McVetty realized that someone had better inform Kelly's parents and quickly walked the hundred-odd steps to their house. The couple had already come outside and met him in their yard where other neighbors were gathered, having heard the police were searching a house on the street.

Richard and Victoria looked terrible. The exhaustion, the hope, the thousand fears had altered them profoundly from the previous day. Yet there was lingering hope in their eyes as the officer approached, though behind it lay dread at what they were about to hear.

McVetty told Richard and Victoria that he had discovered the body of a young girl in the Golubs' basement. Almost instantaneously Victoria began a slow wail that rose in volume until it was a sound that could be heard all along Horton Road. Others standing nearby began sobbing as couples embraced spontaneously and clung to one another. In the midst of the tears and Victoria's profound grief, there were shouts of anger and denial from others. "No!" Richard took his wife into his arms as tears flowed down his cheeks and his husky body shook uncontrollably.

The civilians at the scene were not the only ones so deeply moved. At the police car Brennen had lost her composure entirely. She shouted into the microphone. "We've found a body in a closet! My God, there's a body of a little girl here! Hurry!! We need help! Help us!" She continued in an unbroken stream, rambling, the emotion of the experience plain with every shouted word.

At the Nassau County Police Department, Fifth Precinct Station House, Homicide Squad, in nearby Mineola, Det. Richard Lane heard the call for assistance and noted it was 12:15 P.M. Never before in his career had he heard anyone speak on the police radio in such a way. It was as if a civilian had picked it up. He walked to the squad room and called over to Det. Richard Wells, that day's "squeal man" as the detective on duty was known. The next killing was to be his. Wells was seated at a desk penciling in changes in a homicide report.

"Hey, have you heard what's on the radio? They're screaming. Sounds like they're calling in air strikes on Horton Road in Valley Stream," Lane said with a disbelieving smile. "There's an hysterical woman on the radio saying something about a body in a closet. You better get over there and calm someone down."

Wells was forty-nine years old and had been a detective in Nassau County for thirteen years. A former Army paratrooper, he was a tall, burly man with a mustache and the manner of a stern university professor. He had served Nasssu County with distinction, receiving fourteen commendations for excellent and exceptional police duty; been named detective of the year in 1983; and was recipient of the department's Distinguished Service Medal, the second highest award that could be given to a police officer in Nassau County. He was married to a nurse he had met while working night duty and the couple had six children. He loved homicide and relished every minute he had been a police officer. If there was any element of disappointment in an otherwise exemplary career, it had been the slow pace of his career advancement.

To prevent political interference and to share quality investigations along with the dreary ones, cases were assigned in the Homicide Squad on a strict rotation basis. Because this had been Wells's Saturday for duty, the next murder investigation, no matter what, was his. He had seen more dead bodies than he could easily count, investigated hundreds of homicides, but no case, not one, would have the profound impact on his life as the investigation he was about to begin.

Wells walked the short distance down the hallway to the main office and inquired if a request for the Homicide Squad had been officially received. None had. Wells decided to respond regardless and asked Lane to accompany him as it was standard procedure to work in pairs. While driving to Horton Road the detectives received confirmation of the official request for their participation.

At 12:48 P.M. Lane turned the unmarked car up the one-way street and could see a frenzy of activity ahead. Numerous police cars were already parked haphazardly along the street, uniformed officers were milling around, other detectives were standing about, and between ten and twenty neighbors, civilians as the police called them, were gathered on the sidewalk and in the Golubs' yard. Until now he had thought they would be examining a suicide, since it was not unusual for people to hang themselves in closets.

The two detectives parked down the street, then walked toward the house. Wells eyed the crowd skeptically. The gathering of a handful of people at a murder scene was pretty common, but until today he had never before seen so many. He didn't know it yet but some of those standing there, watching, were members of the Tinyes family.

Wells and Lane were greeted at the front door by an officer with an ashen expression. He said, "I really don't know what we've got, but we have what appears to be a body in the basement, underneath the stairs in a sleeping bag."

"Does she live here? Is she a member of the family?"

"No," the officer said, "we think she is probably the

subject of a missing persons report." He introduced the detectives to John Golub, the owner of the house.

The men walked through the living room, across the dining room, into the kitchen, then down the steps to the basement. "Do you think it could be drugs?" John Golub asked. Detective Wells had no answer. Anything was possible at this point.

Wells first thought as his eyes rested on the basement that it looked as if a bomb had exploded below. Clutter was everywhere and it was impossible to approach the location of the body without disturbing potential evidence. He had seen dirty homes before, most police officers had, but he had never before observed such clutter and chaos in a residence.

John Golub was behind him. "How come you didn't notice the condition of the basement when you were looking down here earlier?" Wells asked.

Golub explained that the basement was in its normal state. In fact, he had just finished cleaning it a few weeks earlier and in the backyard still was a large pile of items he had taken out of the basement but had not as yet thrown away.

"Look around," he said. "The entire house is the same way. My wife is not the best housekeeper. This is the way she keeps it."

Wells made his way cautiously into the basement, then to the closet under the stairs, followed by Lane. His shoes crunched on broken glass. Kneeling down, Wells could see the green sleeping bag and that the zipper had been opened five to six inches. Inside he saw what appeared to be dried blood on human skin. Wells extended his hand then pressed his finger to confirm that what he was seeing was flesh. It was cold to his touch and there was no doubt in his mind that this person was dead.

Now he moved his finger slightly side to side and detected slippage of the skin, a positive indicator that the body had started to decompose. The basement was cool and assuming this was the missing girl he had been told about, her body could normally have been expected to remain firm longer than this. But she had been stuffed into the sleeping bag which held her body's heat and he determined that was the reason decomposition was further along than he would normally have anticipated.

He confirmed for Lane that they had a dead body and the detective told him he would see to the standard notifications. These included the District Attorney's Office, the medical examiner, the Homicide Squad supervisor, the county duty officer, and a police Crime Scene Search Unit to collect physical evidence and take photographs.

It was customary to wait for a medical examiner before proceeding further with the body so Wells went upstairs and spoke to Officer Charney, who briefed him on how he and McVetty had come to discover the body. Wells instructed Charney to remain at the top of the basement stairs and to let no one into the basement until the medical examiner arrived.

Before noon the telephone rang at the Grosse household and Roberta rushed to answer. A girl she knew was crying hysterically and without identifying herself screamed into the telephone, "She's dead! She's dead! I heard it on the radio! She was murdered! They found her in an abandoned house."

Roberta hung up and muttered, "Oh, my God."

* * *

At the top of the stairs at the Golubs' house Wells spoke to McVetty, who advised him of that day's activities leading up to the discovery of the body. Elizabeth Golub was pacing about in the cramped living room wringing her hands. McVetty told Wells the police were present in the house by permission and that no search warrant had as yet been obtained.

Wells nodded his head in comprehension. The sooner a deputy district attorney was on hand to secure the warrant, the better. The Golubs could have a change of heart and order them out at any second.

McVetty said that the oldest son, Robert, was no longer present, but John Jay Golub was upstairs. Kelly's little brother was claiming to have taken a call from a John, a telephone call that had caused her to leave the house the previous afternoon. Wells asked McVetty to come along while he spoke with the teenager. John Jay's father accompanied them to the boy's bedroom.

John Jay appeared to be cooperative as he related the events of the previous day. He had come home from school with two friends, Mick Donnell and Chris Earle, and the trio had played Nintendo. They met with his brother, Robert, for a short time before his older brother went up to his room. The boys left the house not long after that, played some basketball nearby with friends, went to a pizza parlor to eat, then John Jay returned home around 5:00 P.M. Wells left McVetty to continue the interview in detail.

Leaving the house, Wells noticed that one of the upstairs bedrooms did not have a door and made a mental note of it. A sheet was draped across the doorway. On the main floor he also noticed there was nowhere to sit. Every chair, every possible space, was occupied with clothing and various debris piled on top. The dining-room table had two to three feet of clothing and papers on it. There was no visible work area in the kitchen.

Wells stepped through the front door. Outside the day had become overcast. The clear weather with its promise of spring was now heavy with humidity and an impending cold rain. Officers had spread the bright yellow police-line tape, pushing back reporters, neighbors, and curious police officers to secure the location. The crowd Wells had seen when he arrived earlier was swelling as word spread throughout the neighborhood.

Roberta's father had instructed her not to answer the telephone anymore that day. He was unable to reach the Tinyeses by phone, and instead received a call from the parents of one of his daughter's friends. It was a long, one-sided conversation as he listened intently, Roberta following him closely as her father paced back and forth trying to distance himself from her so she would not overhear what he was hearing.

"What, Dad? What?" she asked repeatedly. When the call was finished he was grim and asked his daughter to please sit, he had something to tell her.

"Just tell me," she said. "I just want to hear it."

"Roberta, I'm sorry. Kelly died."

Roberta screamed at her father. "You are such a liar. How could you lie to me! Why would you ever say that!"

She began sobbing and her father pulled her against

him, squeezing her so tight she thought she would burst, holding her as if to be certain she was really there, knowing that as long as Roberta was in his arms nothing could ever happen to her.

Shortly after 1:00 P.M. the Crime Scene Search Unit arrived on Horton Road and Wells briefed them on the situation. The basement would likely be filled with physical evidence, but the working conditions were nearly impossible. The investigators had to be very, very careful. When the men saw the basement for themselves they looked at Wells as if he were kidding. Work methodically in that?

Wells ordered that a series of photographs be taken before anything further was done, in order to preserve the location of objects and description of the basement prior to the crime-scene detectives starting work. He also instructed that photographs of the exterior of the house be taken as well.

In Nassau County such crime-scene teams were comprised of specially trained police officers. In other jurisdictions civilian police employees performed the work. Present on this team were two officers supervised by Det. William Steinbeck, a twenty-one-year veteran of the police department, and on the Crime Scene Search Unit for the last four years. He was of average build with black hair that was balding in front and wore a mustache.

Steinbeck took the exterior shots first. Then the basement was lit by a steady series of flashes as he snapped a seemingly unending series of photographs. Finally the three officer technicians knelt down and began the painstaking task of searching for clues. A usual crime scene could be searched and logged in a few hours, certainly in no more than a day. The task ahead of these men would last nearly around the clock for almost two weeks.

Just as the technicians were turning to their task, Dr. Lone Thanning, a deputy medical examiner, arrived accompanied by the tour medical examiner who customarily handled death by natural causes. Thanning was a slender Swede in her mid-thirties who still spoke English with a distinctive accent and often wore wooden shoes as she did today. At 2:00 P.M. the two doctors and Wells descended to the basement to examine the body.

Wells pulled the sleeping bag carefully from the closet and laid it on the basement floor. Beneath it was a wad of white lace curtains saturated with blood that had leaked from the bag. Beneath the curtains was a pool of gathered blood and lying in the liquid was a knife. Wells looked closely. It was a well-worn, long-bladed bayonet, probably from the First World War.

Turning his attention to the bag he slowly unzipped it, careful not to touch the zipper on its flat surface so as not to erase any possible fingerprints. When the zipper was fully extended he now parted the bag and from inside came the foul smell of rotting flesh and fecal matter. As the odor burst from the opened sleeping bag, Thanning, who had seen thousands of dead bodies by this point in her career, turned abruptly away and threw her hand to her face. "My God!" she exclaimed.

In the jaded closed circle of the Homicide Squad, Wells was known as the "squad man" for his hardened, cynical demeanor. His father abandoned his family when he was still a toddler and his mother had managed to raise him and his younger sister working as a domestic. Wells had been supporting himself since he was fourteen years old. To say that he had seen it all would be an understatement of monumental proportions. Nothing should have shocked him at this point in his career, nothing, he would have said with confidence, could still move him.

So it was that when he exposed the body of this young girl and looked first at the face, he saw with vivid clarity the lovely face of his own daughter. The vision pulled him up sharply. He shook his head for an instant and blinked his eyes, then focused on the face in front of him. It was, of course, not his daughter. What he saw instead was scarcely recognizable as human.

The face was purple, blackened in places from massive bruising, and Wells could not imagine how many blows it would take to destroy a face and cause such damage.

The body was of a teenage female. Her throat had been hideously slit with a cut so deep it extended nearly to her backbone. Large patches of hair had been pulled from her scalp. He could see a tuft by her torso, another by a thigh. Lying in the bag was a bra that appeared to have been dipped in a vat of blood. It was knotted and appeared to be fashioned into a choking device. Clasped in the knot was a clump of hair.

Even more shocking than the condition of the face was the body itself. The skin of the victim was layered with bruises. Whoever had killed this girl had done so with an excess of violence.

But what caught Wells's attention and held it transfixed was not the face, the blood, or the massive bruising. From the top of her chest to below her vagina the body had been slit and laid open, exposing her internal organs. The breasts were intact but were so covered with blood Wells had trouble determining their condition. And as he examined the body more carefully he could see lacerations, long and shallow cuts, latticing the upper portion of the body, for reasons he could not imagine. The lower portion of the legs were contained in a trash bag. He could see a whole box of them nearby. In all the deaths he had seen prior to this, he had never before observed such damage, not even on a body struck by a train.

Whoever had done this was a tremendously powerful person Wells reasoned. He had seen John Jay upstairs and suspected his two friends were of about the same age and modest build. No boy in his early teens was physically capable of this.

Lane had been watching events from the stairs along with another detective. "I don't think a fourteen-year-old could do this. Find me the other brother," Wells instructed. Someone older had done this. Someone stronger. Lane nodded his head and went up the stairs to give instructions that Robert Golub be located and brought in for questioning.

Leaning down Wells could detect blistering as well as slippage of the skin. This occurred when the fluids had largely drained from a body and indicated to him that the body was in an even more advanced state of decomposition than he had initially suspected. The effect of the sleeping bag had been to hold not just the heat of the body at the moment it was placed into the bag, but to retain the heat generated by decomposition and in effect to create a small oven.

Wells now carefully examined the edge and general

condition of the bayonet and could tell at once that while some of the cuts may have been caused by this weapon, almost certainly given that it was here with the body, many of the cuts were inconsistent with the blade. Something else had been used.

Wells stepped back to allow Thanning to conduct her examination and at 2:15 P.M. she officially pronounced the victim to be dead.

To fix the time of death it was necessary to establish the body temperature. Wells had determined from observation that the body had gone into rigor mortis and was coming out of it now. That process took anywhere from twelve to twenty hours. The temperature reading would be a more accurate measurement as the formulas for the rate of the loss of body heat had been worked out by medical examiners years before. Even the sleeping bag would present no problem.

Wells moved the body and inserted the thermometer into the victim's anus, but it immediately fell out. Looking closer Wells realized the young girl had been slit through the vagina across the lower portion of her body to the anus. He reinserted the thermometer and held the flesh together with his fingers to obtain a temperature reading.

Additional photographs were taken now. Wells snapped several Polaroids which he retained for the immediate use of the investigation. Someone was going to have to tell him if this was Kelly Ann Tinyes, and he wasn't about to ask anyone to come down here to do it.

While the body was further examined by Thanning, then readied for transportation to the medical examiners for autopsy, Wells went outside for fresh air, to cleanse himself of the odor of death. He found the general condition of the house and of the basement to be claustrophobic.

It was odd how normal the house seemed from the outside; not really any different in appearance and care from the others. You can never tell from the outside, he thought, just what it is like behind the walls.

John Golub joined him briefly. "Was it drugs?" he asked.

Wells looked at him and recalled the carnage he had just seen. "No," he replied. "It wasn't drugs." Golub stood a moment as if contemplating what that meant, then turned and went back into the house.

Wells had an immediate problem with identification. There was a missing girl and down the street a family already grieving. In some circumstances he would have asked a family member to look at the body, but that was out of the question. How could he ask anyone who had loved the girl downstairs to see her in this condition? An officer approached and told him that a Mr. McGoldrick, a lawyer and friend of the Golub family wished to speak to him.

Wells groaned inwardly. In the early 1980s two Nassau County detectives had escorted Herbert Rogers, a murder suspect, into custody after receiving specific orders from the court not to question him unless his lawyer was present. En route, the suspect spoke spontaneously of his religious beliefs and expressed remorse as well as concern that the woman he had murdered would not receive a proper burial. By coincidence, and no doubt the impetus for his comments, the men were driving past the location where he had dumped the body. The officers asked if he wanted to waive his right to an attorney and tell them about it. He did, made a statement, and led the officers to the body.

From this case the New York State Court of Appeals, the highest appellate court in the state, held that once a lawyer was involved in a case absolutely no questioning, even voluntary speaking, could take place unless he was present, nor could the accused waive his right to an attorney. The conviction was reversed.

Even in these days of forensic science the reality for most police officers was no different than it had ever been. Most cases were solved by confession. The Rogers decision made their job that much more difficult in the State of New York. Now a lawyer wanted to see the Golubs.

Wells was unaware of any murder conviction ever being obtained since the Rogers decision when a lawyer entered the picture before a confession had been given. This was a disaster.

Four

Before speaking to McGoldrick, Wells was advised that deputy district attorney Dan Cotter was on the scene. Cotter, a gregarious, flamboyant career prosecutor, was popular with the homicide detectives. He was single, drove a flashy Corvette, but more importantly, had an unbroken string of convictions in murder cases. The two men spoke briefly and Wells explained they were present on a signed consent order. Now a lawyer had arrived.

Search warrants are issued by judges, and while a procedure existed to obtain them on weekends, it was not easy or quick. In the meantime Cotter suggested the gathering of physical evidence wait until they had a warrant and Wells agreed. Cotter went next door to the Stonels' house where he worked on the affidavit. When it was ready two assisting officers were dispatched to begin the laborious process of obtaining a search warrant on a Saturday.

William McGoldrick was angry since the uniformed officers had been refusing to let him into the house. He explained to Wells that he was a friend of the Golub family and that he would like to enter the Golubs' residence to speak with them. McGoldrick went on to explain that he was here to be of assistance, that he was a neighbor who lived not far away, and that he had once been a New York state police officer.

"What hat are you going to wear here? Are you here as a friend of the family, as a neighbor, or as a lawyer?" Wells asked. He had to know.

"I really don't know. I don't want to get involved in this necessarily, but I feel I owe it to talk to the family," McGoldrick replied.

Wells had never worked a crime scene like this before. Usually the entire house at the site of a order was sealed off until the examination of the house was completed. In this case only the basement was safeguarded. He had people wandering around the other two levels doing—God knew what.

Now Wells had a lawyer on his hands. He told McGoldrick to go ahead. As he did a police command van arrived and began to set up operation in front of the house. Such vans were used at crime scenes like this to give officers a place to speak in confidence and to secure lines of communication.

While they waited on the search warrant Wells issued instructions to officers to canvass the neighborhood and to begin taking statements. He sent a pair to locate Donnell and Earle, then dispatched his best interviewer, Det. Jack Sharkey, into the house to speak to John Jay. It was likely the younger Golub had made the telephone call that summoned Kelly to the Golubs' house, as it was he who knew Kelly. One of the young girl's friends had told officers that John Jay had been "sweet" on Kelly for years. It was probable that John Jay had been lying to him earlier, and for now that made him a suspect. There was no evidence that only one person had committed this murder.

As Wells was doing this he was advised that members of the Tinyes family wanted to enter the Golubs' house in an attempt to identify the body. One of these was Robert Player who, Wells was informed, was acting as family spokesman and was also a former police officer.

Wells spoke to Player who explained that he wanted to make himself available to the police in any way he could. Wells extracted a Polaroid photograph he had taken of the victim, careful to cover the body with his hand and asked if Player would try to make an identification from the picture of the head. He cautioned that this would be a gruesome sight. Player nodded his head in understanding. When he looked at the photograph his lips pursed in a tight line and he said, "Yes, that was Kelly Ann Tinyes."

Wells instructed two detectives to accompany Player back to the Tinyeses' home and advise them of the positive identification. Television camera crews had established themselves in front of the Tinyeses' house by this time. When Player told Kelly's parents that he had seen a photograph of their daughter and that there was absolutely no doubt that Kelly was dead, the screams from the house could be heard through the walls and were recorded on videotape. Even Wells, standing five houses down, could hear the "bloodcurdling" cries. *My God,* he thought. *My God.*

McGoldrick, looking distraught, came back outside to talk to Wells after speaking with the Golubs. "You've got a tough one, huh?"

"Yeah, a bad one," Wells answered. "Let me show you how bad it is." He took the Polaroid out he had just shown Player only this time he did not cover up the body.

"Oh, my God," McGoldrick looked away quickly from the photograph then he said, "Let me tell you something, Detective. Nobody in this house did this."

"What are you saying to me?" The Golubs' daughter, Adele, had arrived not long before this, accompanied by her fiancé. The only of the Golub family not in the house was the older son, Robert.

"Well . . ."

"Who do you represent?" Wells asked.

"Everybody in this house. The Golub family."

"What about Robert?"

"Do you see him here?"

"No, I don't," Wells said.

"Then I don't represent him." The lawyer leaned closer and spoke in a hushed voice. "Let me tell you something. John Jay didn't do it." Before Wells could ask what he meant by that, McGoldrick had turned on his heel and walked back into the house.*

Chief of the Nassau County Homicide Squad was John Nolan, a stout, redheaded, twenty-two-year veteran police officer with over four hundred homicide investigations, and supervisor of the squad's twenty-five employees for the last two years. When he was named to head the squad, the first detective he had asked to have

---

*Conversations between McGoldrick and Wells are taken from Wells' recollection. McGoldrick subsequently rendered a different account.

assigned was Richard Wells, his old partner from their plainclothes days. Wells had been in line to be assignedto homicide for several years, but had been refused because of a personality conflict with the former chief.

There are different breeds of cops. Wells typified the traditional street cop. A keen observer of people, skilled interrogator, hardworking upholder of the law, with disdain for liberal courts and judges. He not only possessed rough edges, he relished them. Around the squad he was known as a ball buster, and if a detective couldn't take the razzing, then to hell with him. He had the respect of nearly every man he worked with, and the friendship of very few. John Nolan was one of the latter group.

Nolan was another kind of cop. Hardworking, dedicated, but schooled and articulate in promoting himself. He tested well on the civil-service exams and had been named to head the Homicide Squad while still a sergeant, something unheard of in Nassau County. The appointment had come in large part because of his smooth handling of the press in previous murder investigations. Though the department had a press-relations officer, reporters had formed a natural affinity for Nolan, who quickly mastered the art of giving a reporter a story for the day without saying more than he should.

Nolan's promotion to chief of homicide had not been equally well received by others in the squad who considered themselves more deserving. He had worked hard in the past twenty-seven months to be accepted and to bring long overdue changes to the squad. He had instituted the rotation system of case assignments, two-men investigative teams, and the use of consent forms for voluntary searches. He still had his detractors in the squad, but increasingly he had gained the respect of the men he supervised.

Yet beneath the contrasting demeanors Nolan and Wells were very much alike. More importantly they trusted one another. And in the months to come that trust would come to mean more than comradery or even friendship.

Now a lieutenant, Nolan was drum major in the police department's bagpipe band and was participating in a pre-St. Patrick's Day parade when his beeper sounded. "Ah, someone died," one of the others commented. Nolan was informed of the discovery of the body in the Golubs' house. Not wanting to arrive at the scene of a murder investigation in an Irish kilt, he rushed home to change, then drove to Valley Stream. As a consequence he did not arrive until after 5:00 P.M. Wells was still waiting for a search warrant as teams of officers met with him in the command van and briefed him on what they were learning from their canvass of the neighborhood.

The situation Nolan found was the worst set of circumstances a policeman faced conducting an investigation, and he could readily understand Wells's distress. McGoldrick was now present in the house. The Golubs had been discussing events among themselves since the body was discovered. Standard police procedure was to separate all potential sources so that such a pooling of information did not take place, but that had not been possible in this case.

Sharkey was the most cerebral of Wells's officers and was well suited for his role, though in this situation he faced an impossible task. He spoke to the Golubs as a group since the lawyer would not let them be separated, and reconstructed the events of the previous day. There was not even a proper location in the house in which to conduct the interview. People were sitting wherever they could squeeze into a spot, with piles of clothing pressed up against them or moved to the floor.

Sharkey spoke to John Jay first and had him repeat the information he had given officers earlier that day. When Sharkey asked him directly about the telephone call, John Jay again denied making it. He said that the police had ways of checking on those things so why bother him. He also told Sharkey that by the end of the day the police would know what had happened to Kelly and the circumstances around it. Sharkey asked what he meant by that but John Jay shrugged the question off.

Sharkey learned that on Friday, John Golub, the father, had left for his Getty service station at 6:45 A.M. where he worked all day with his staff. Elizabeth had taken John Jay to school at 7:40 that morning as was her custom, then had driven to her own job where she also remained for the day.

John Jay, who was chronically truant, managed to remain at school on Friday and arrived at his house just before three P.M accompanied by two friends, Mick Donnell and Chris Earle. His older brother Robert, who had been unemployed since the previous summer, was just taking mail from the mailbox. John Jay claimed he played Nintendo with his friends, then at 3:45 P.M. had left with them for a basketball game at a nearby court.

John Golub quit work to run errands at 4:45 P.M. and spotted John Jay at a bus stop. He picked him up and the two drove home, arriving at 4:55 P.M., just moments before the start of John Golub's favorite television show, *T.J. Hooker.*

Elizabeth Golub went grocery shopping following work and was home preparing dinner by 5:30 P.M. She dished out individual portions for her family at about six P.M. and as was their habit each member of the family ate alone in his bedroom. She recalled that she had to awaken Robert from a deep sleep to call him to dinner.

John Jay was grounded and his father believed his youngest son had stayed in that night, but in fact John Jay had gone out with friends for a few hours. He was back home and in bed by 10:15 P.M. Robert had gone drinking at a bar with a friend, Paul Zerella, and was back before eleven P.M. The father went to bed at nine P.M. and his wife retired at eleven P.M.

John Jay's answers did not appear forthcoming to Sharkey and from time to time he pressed John Jay about his evasive responses to his questions, but the teenager grew even less cooperative. In the presence of his parents and the lawyer, he became increasingly cocky. Several of his answers had been smart-ass and as a consequence Sharkey's suspicion toward him heightened.

Officers arrived at the scene with the search warrant at about six P.M. The technicians, who had been on standby, now painstakingly started gathering evidence from the Golubs' basement and from the house in general. Since Kelly had been discovered naked, of particular interest to investigators was the young girl's clothing. Their task was unbelievably difficult because of the extraordinarily cluttered interior of the entire house. The backyard was filled with trash and contained a large pyramid of items taken from the general cleaning of the basement about two weeks before.

Nolan briefly examined the basement and the upstairs of the house. He made a point to stand in the bedrooms of the two boys and carefully searched for any sign of Satanism or witchcraft. He had attended several training seminars on the phenomenon, and having learned of the destruction of Kelly's body wanted to satisfy himself this was not cult-related. He found nothing.

As Nolan walked through the living room, he could not believe the impossible situation Sharkey was facing in trying to interview John Jay. The boy was in control of the situation, not the other way around. It was very unlikely the detective was going to learn anything this way.

Nolan ignored Sharkey, conveying with his body language that he did not want to be introduced to anyone. Detectives routinely avoided situations by saying they would have to check with their boss. Nolan did not want to be identified as the officer in charge because the lawyer would ask him when the police were going to clear out and leave his clients in peace. He needed more time.

Outside the sun was just setting behind the leafless trees and Nolan stood in the yard for a moment to watch it. This was, he thought, a very unusual house. Then he went to the command van to wait for the discovery of more evidence.

It was dusk outside and growing darker. Officers erected floodlights in the basement and in a circle surrounding the house. A steady, cold rain now fell and water glistened off the yellow police tape marking the crime scene. A crush of media had already arrived and the television crews had erected their own floodlights, adding to the surreal quality of the scene.

When Kelly's body was carried from the Golubs' house, a large crowd of neighbors was gathered. Tears flowed and people held one another for comfort. It was not the usual shabby scene at a murder site and only reinforced for Nolan how different this situation was.

The previous December a Long Island husband had murdered his wife on Christmas Eve. The investigation had become a media circus until the man had finally confessed and led officers to her body. Looking at the crush of reporters Nolan sensed immediately that this was going to be a case of similar fascination to the media and public. He was glad to have Wells running the investigation. Wells hated reporters as much as he hated liberal judges and could be counted on not to leak anything.

Nolan gave statements to the press as usual. If he didn't the reporters would hound his men relentlessly trying to solicit a comment. At an impromptu press conference he reminded the reporters that the Golubs had consented to the search of their home. "They are bewildered and shocked by this," he said. "They have no idea who let the girl in." He added, "The adults were very cooperative in this search and at this time we don't have any particular suspects, but we are confining our search for her clothes to the area. We won't know anything about the girl's death until an autopsy is completed."

It wasn't much and it certainly wasn't enough to satisfy the reporters, who already were hearing reports of the extent of the mutilation that had taken place, but it was all Nolan was going to give them.

In the basement Steinbeck and his officers were doing their best to cope with the situation. A single drop of blood or sample of hair could be crucial in solving the case, but there was so much litter it was nearly impossible to work any piece of evidence without moving something else.

Steinbeck and the others moved cautiously through the sea of debris, snapping additional photographs of everything he thought required preserving. Several times he zeroed in on what appeared to be bloodstains. He had taken a series of shots of the closet before Kelly was removed, then he gathered samples of cardboard, paper, clothing, scraps of carpeting, a silver button, and a card table, all of which appeared to have been bloodied. He placed an old framed photograph of three young children into a plastic bag because he could observe splattered blood on it.

Wells was the focal point for information gathered by detectives as well as the commanding officer of the investigation. The entire resources of the Homicide Squad, indeed of the Nassau County Police Department, were quite literally now at his disposal. It was Nolan's job to acquire those resources as needed, to hold the media at bay and to screen Wells from the inevitable pressure that would come from senior command in the police department.

The full magnitude of what had taken place in the Golubs' basement had not yet been published, but Nolan knew that it soon would be, and once that occurred he and Wells would be placed under extraordinary pressure to produce a killer or killers. Nolan had seen it before and feared he was about to witness it in a fashion without precedent in his experience.

* * *

Detectives located Robert in a van with Zerella a few blocks away from his house. They observed the young men a short time, then followed the van to the back of a movie theater. There they pulled it over. Asked to come to the police precinct for questioning, Robert casually inquired if this was about his outstanding traffic tickets. One of the detectives said, "No, it's about Kelly Ann Tinyes."

At the command van Wells ordered that a serologist respond to the scene since large amounts of blood, some of it still pooled, were being located in the basement. If the serologist could gather enough samples, he would run various blood tests that could effectively determine whose blood was at the murder scene, or, at the least, eliminate suspects. In the case of a knife attack such as this, it was not unusual for the killer or killers to have a self-inflicted injury. If that had happened then they might get lucky enough to find the killer's blood as well.

Such blood samples were customarily taken by the Crime Scene Search Unit, but in this case Wells wanted the serologist who would actually perform the tests to be present and collect the samples for himself. Bringing in a specialist like this in major cases was a constant source of friction between homicide detectives and the technicians, but Wells wanted the best men possible working the scene and to hell with bad feelings.

Wells also learned that Robert had waived his right to an attorney and was answering questions the detectives were putting to him at the station. He was advised that both Donnell and Earle were also being questioned there. Wells left the detectives at the Golubs' residence to continue gathering evidence while he drove to the police precinct in Mineola.

When Wells arrived one of the detectives who had questioned Robert Golub's friend Paul Zerella, briefed him on what he had learned. According to Zerella, he had picked Robert up at his house Friday night at about nine P.M. They bought marijuana, which they smoked, had gone drinking in a bar, then eaten junk food at a convenience market. He had dropped Robert off at his house at one A.M. During the evening Robert had never mentioned the name of Kelly Ann Tinyes nor once related anything that had happened in the house. Zerella was allowed to leave.

The detectives questioning the two juveniles introduced Wells to Mick Donnell and his parents as well as to Chris Earle and his mother and father. The two youths had been separated and were being questioned individually by juvenile officers in the presence of their parents. The story they were telling was essentially the same, but there were differences. Only extended questioning would eventually allow the detectives to learn what the boys knew.

Wells sat in on the interviews and asked an occasional question. Primarily he wanted to listen to what the boys were saying to see if it had the ring of truth, if their manner was cooperative or evasive. And in both cases he observed their hands carefully for any sign of trauma. It was not likely that the murderer had escaped an assault of this magnitude without some injury. On the hands of the two teenagers he saw no cuts, no abrasions, nothing. Earle was even wearing a cast on one forearm. There was no sign of blood, no trauma of any kind to it.

Wells walked to the interview room of the Homicide

Squad. Before entering he was briefed and informed that Robert Golub denied seeing Kelly the previous day, indeed denied seeing her for several weeks. Asked to give his fingerprints and hair samples, Robert had readily done both. His manner was cooperative and he seemed to be telling the truth.

Robert was ruggedly built, with broad shoulders and powerful arms developed from years of weight lifting. He was proud of the fact that he could bench-press three hundred pounds, nearly twice his body weight, yet he stood not much over five feet tall.

Robert was calm and composed as he related he had awakened at ten or ten-thirty that morning. He had eaten breakfast, then walked to the nearby King Kullen, where he bought a muscle magazine which he read most of the day when he wasn't watching television in his room. He had only left the house again in the afternoon to retrieve the mail and recalled that shortly after that his brother and two friends Robert did not know arrived.

They went into the kitchen while Robert read the mail, then walked upstairs to his brother's room. Robert followed them up, lay on his bed, and resumed watching television. John Jay and friends were listening to the stereo in his brother's room. Asked what the boys had talked about Robert said he could not understand them, but he could tell they were smoking marijuana. Asked again what he had done in the house, Robert replied that he had remained in his room watching television. After a while he no longer heard his brother and friends talking and assumed they had gone downstairs. Not much later Robert had drifted off to sleep.

He was awakened at 6:30 that night by John Jay who told him there was a telephone call from a girl for him, but Robert declined to take it. At 7:00 his mother told him dinner was ready and he had eaten in his room, consuming a meal of fish cakes and spaghetti along with three beers. At 8:30 P.M. he had gone out with a friend to a few bars. He returned late, around midnight, after everyone else in the house was in bed.

Robert told the officers he had not seen Kelly at the house or anywhere else, though he knew she called his younger brother two or three times a day. He said he had no idea where she could be.

"Robert, this isn't about a missing person," one of the officers told him. "We are investigating her murder. When was the last time you were in the basement?"

Robert considered the question for a moment, then said he had last been in the basement about two weeks before. Wells could see why some of the interviewing detectives were persuaded by the glib young man. There was an earnestness in his manner, a perceived eagerness to be cooperative that seemed to confirm he was not the killer.

John Jay's two friends, Donnell and Earle, had been interviewed at length by now and Wells went back to hear if their stories had altered in any way. They argued they had nothing to do with Kelly's murder nor had John Jay who had been with them nearly every minute. Telephone records confirmed that a call had been made from the Golubs' house to the Tinyeses' home, but they denied making it, as did John Jay and Robert.

Such speedy confirmation from the telephone company was something brand-new to Wells, though within a few years it would become routine. As the newest telephone technology on Long Island had come on-line, the very first area to receive it had been Valley Stream. Only in this area at the time could the telephone company obtain a record of calls. When Nolan had been informed he took it as a good omen. Maybe, just maybe, God was smiling on this investigation.

Donnell acknowledged to officers they had been smoking marijuana that afternoon though Earle was admitting nothing. Both boys agreed that Robert had his stereo on and was listening to rock music. John Jay had snuck into his brother's room to turn it to full blast. It had been impossible to hear anything other than the steady beat of the drums and howling of the singers.

Speaking of John Jay, Donnell said, "He didn't have time to call anyone. He didn't have time to answer the door. He didn't have time to kill anyone. He didn't have time to do anything." Donnell said that at one point a dazed and seemingly confused Robert had stuck his head into the room and demanded to know who had turned on his stereo. He seemed unconvinced when the boys said he had and John Jay didn't volunteer that he had been the one to turn it up.

Of the pair Donnell appeared the most forthcoming. His family had the appearance of being all-American and Wells could easily picture them on a magazine cover. Earle's situation impressed Wells as quite different. The boy was clearly afraid of his father and his story came out only as the officers dragged it from him. Earle still insisted they had been playing Nintendo.

Wells returned to Robert and watched the smooth talker spin his tale of innocence. Wells was gaining confidence now in his case. And when Robert told a particularly effective story, Wells only had to look at his hands, to glance a moment at the abrasions and cuts he could clearly see. He wondered how Robert was going to explain them.

Five

Officer Wayne Birdsall, the serologist assigned to the scientific bureau, had arrived at the scene shortly after Kelly's body had been removed. A dark-haired, straight-backed, handsome man with a direct pleasant manner, he was known to be methodical and conscientious in working any crime scene.

He began his assignment by examining the exterior of the Golubs' house. He searched the sidewalks, street, backyard, and lawn as well as the neighbors' sidewalk and driveways and had found no traces of blood. Next he examined the interior of the house, starting at the front door, working his way through the living room, into the dining room, and on to the kitchen. He noticed the generally cluttered condition of the house, but again found no bloodstains.

Then he checked the landing to the stairs from the kitchen which led into the basement. He found no blood there or in the stairwell. But once he reached the carpet of the basement floor, it all changed. Suddenly he could see stains in many places. He followed a trail of blood which led him to the closet under the stairs and inside observed a large puddle of blood and the bloodied curtains on which the sleeping bag with Kelly had been thrown. Now he could spot stains on the wood paneling and molding, some of it still a bright red, indicating it was fresh.

Next he examined the ten-foot-by-ten-foot room to the rear of the basement across from where Kelly's body had been discovered. And based on blood splatterings he found on the walls and other evidence, he determined that Kelly had been murdered in this room. Three pools of blood were apparent on the floor, so fresh they had not as yet dried.

Birdsall found more blood in the basement, blood on the back side of the doorknob of the back room where Kelly had been killed. He found blood on the carpet, blood on paper, blood and more blood almost everywhere he looked.

One of the items Elizabeth Golub had acquired from her frequent garage sale excursions was a box containing four attaché cases. Birdsall had methodically worked his way across the basement, collecting and marking samples as he did, and by that evening had found his way to the box of attaché cases, located on the far side of the basement near the room where Kelly had been murdered.

He first observed that the cardboard appeared to be resting in water. Closer examination showed the liquid to be blood. Looking more closely at the box he observed the distinctive reddish-brown stains of blood. He took a series of photographs, then slowly opened the box.

One of the four attaché cases was still wrapped in its shipping cocoon of plastic. On the top of two of the cases Birdsall could detect again reddish-brown stains that appeared to be smeared blood. The photographs and examination of the exterior of the box and cases for fingerprints took nearly four hours so it was not until evening that officers opened the first case.

Inside was a turtleneck, two white sneakers, some white tissue paper, white panties, two black socks, a white T-shirt, and black jeans. All of them were marked with blood; some were soaked in it. The items matched those of the clothes Kelly was last known to have worn.

Inside the second case Birdsall discovered a bloodied green sweater and beneath it a brown leather jacket, identical to Kelly's. The third case contained a blue tablecloth soaked in blood and a piece of plastic. Every item was tagged and placed in a container for preservation.

On the floor not far from the box of attaché cases the investigator spotted another piece of glass, different from the others strewn about the basement. It was smeared with the reddish-brown stain of blood. It was placed into a plastic evidence pouch.

Driving back to the Golubs' residence after midnight while the interviews of the boys and Robert continued, Wells cleared his mind of any opinions he was forming and looked at the case afresh. He was faced with unappealing possibilities. The first was that Kelly had been murdered elsewhere, then smuggled into the Golubs' basement through its locked side door and concealed in the closet. Given the amount of blood apparent throughout the basement as well as the fact that three separate witnesses had seen Kelly enter the front door, that was highly unlikely. In their working parlance officers were now referring to the basement as the murder room.

The second possibility was that she had been murdered by a combination of the people present in the house at the time of her death which he estimated to have been between three and eight P.M. That meant Mr. and Mrs. Golub, their sons and their youngest son's two friends, in some mix, had committed the crime. That also seemed highly unlikely. This was not a gang he was dealing with. The generations were wrong and there was no evidence to suggest such a diverse group had acted in concert. In the case of the parents the idea was especially unlikely since they had readily agreed to the search. By applying that logic, however, even John Jay was free of complicity, since McVetty said he had urged his mother to sign the search consent form.

The third possibility was that just one or perhaps two of those in the house had murdered Kelly and hidden her body, and that no one else then present in the house knew about it. But it was not likely one or two of those in the house had committed the murder. Though the Golubs' house had three levels, it was not especially large. It was highly improbable anyone there could murder Kelly and no one else know of it.

There was more to consider. Kelly's face had been nearly destroyed when she was beaten, and experience had taught that murderers who know the victim tended to smash faces, strangers don't. So it was likely whoever did this had known her. This placed the focus of their inquiry on John Jay as there was no evidence that Robert knew the girl.

This was an exercise that Wells had followed many times, one he would be doing again in just a few hours as new facts came to light. Eventually the speculation would be stripped away until what was left was the truth, and with the truth Wells would have his killer.

As soon as he arrived back on Horton Road, Wells was summoned into the basement to see the attaché cases and clothes. He noticed that each attaché case was lined with foam that had been cut out in a series of small circles. No one had any idea what they were for.

The methodical search of the Golubs' basement continued throughout the night. Wells explained to John Golub that he would issue him a receipt for everything they were taking away for examination.

"I've got a large collection of antique pocket watches that are very valuable," Golub said.

"I haven't seen or heard of any so far," Wells replied.

"There are some in my bedroom and there's some downstairs in attaché cases."

Wells thought about that for a moment, remembering the empty circles cut in the foam, then said, "I don't think you have a collection anymore."

As the investigation continued members of the Golub family answered fresh questions for detectives. Routine procedure required that each prepare a written statement.

Shortly before one A.M. Birdsall called out for the others and Nolan, who had remained at the scene. The officer had discovered a print on the molding of the closet where Kelly's body had been hidden. He had conducted a field test which confirmed that it had been made in blood. The latent print was located in such a position that it was likely whoever had placed Kelly's body into the closet had braced himself by leaning against the wall.

Nolan could scarcely contain his excitement. It was unusual to find a legible fingerprint at a murder scene and almost unheard of to locate one in blood. God was smiling on this investigation for certain he told the others and confidently predicted they would have the killer within three hours. Whoever was a match for that print was their man. Nolan told Birdsall to remove the molding and rush it to the laboratory where the print would be matched to those they had taken of Robert, whom he believed to be the killer.

Nolan informed Wells about the print and he shared his enthusiasm. Wells's suspicion toward Robert had returned when he had finished his evaluation of the case. Of the four who had been inside the Golubs home at the time of the killing, only Robert had been alone for any significant period of time. He had also remained with Robert long enough to hear him being asked about the small cuts and abrasions on his hands. Robert had explained he had nicked himself changing weights. The cuts were small and it was impossible to tell how old they were.

The print was changing everything for Wells and Nolan. By now Robert had been talking for four or five hours, and it was time for inconsistencies in his story to start developing. Wells decided to return to take a more active role in the questioning. Confessions were his specialty and with this new piece of evidence he was satisfied that Robert Golub would crack.

It was just after one A.M. when Nolan left for the precinct with Wells not far behind him. What had at first seemed to be a nearly insurmountable task of painstakingly gathering forensic evidence had turned into an open-and-shut case. He knew that Robert was insisting he had not seen Kelly for some time or even been in the basement. At the precise moment when it could be used to maximum advantage, Wells would drop his fresh print on him; Robert would fall apart; and the

case would be solved. Nolan had done it himself; he
had seen Wells do it many, many times.

Nolan located the coffeepot as he waited for Wells,
planning to step in on the interviewing of Robert in just
a few minutes. The match of the latent print against
Robert's would only take a short time. This promised
to be an unexpectedly satisfying ending to a very gruesome case.

Instead, a worried detective approached Nolan as he
entered his office. "I've got bad news, John," he said.
"The print was smudged in transit."

Nolan could not believe what he was hearing. His detectives handled thousands of prints a year without difficulty. Now he was being told the most important print
his squad had ever uncovered had been obliterated in transit? He exploded. How could such a thing happen? My
God, think what the defense would make of it if the print
had been smeared beyond use. It would taint the entire
investigation. The killer was down the hall in an interrogation room. He had waived his rights. All they had to
do was lower the hammer, and this man was telling him
the crucial bit of evidence had been destroyed? Nolan felt
as if he had been kicked in the stomach.

"There's still the photographs," the detective suggested hopefully.

"Sure," Nolan said. A technician had taken photographs of the print before removing it just in case something like this happened. "Who knows what condition
they'll be in." Though photographs were often used to
make the actual match, Nolan was afraid to be optimis-

tic at this point. He could just hope that the print was still usable.

Wells learned of the trouble a few minutes later and could scarcely believe what had taken place. Detective Sergeant Edward Nawrocki, Commanding Officer of the Latent Print Section, and a thirty-five-year veteran of the police force, was at the precinct and had taken control of the molding and just maybe he could come up with something.

Robert was still talking, however, and that was a plus. Wells entered the room and examined his suspect once again. He could understand why so many of the detectives questioning Robert were uncertain of his involvement, but watching the young man answering questions Wells noticed behavior he thought the others were missing.

Robert never showed any emotion. He should be angry or upset or teary-eyed. Instead, he was stoic, flat and methodical. He was sticking to his story and some of the detectives found that persuasive, but the story was so simple a child could remember it.

And there was something else. Robert knew Kelly Ann Tinyes, a friend of his brother, a neighborhood girl he acknowledged having seen from a distance, had been murdered in his basement. Yet he never spoke of the murder itself. "I know something bad happened in my house," he said many times, "but I don't know anything about it."

Something bad? That was putting the best possible light on the monstrous event.

Ask an uninvolved person what he or she thinks should happen to a killer and they say he should be executed, or spend the rest of his life in prison, or that he should receive help. Ask a killer what he or she thinks should happen and they reply, "Things happen all the time. Why ask me?" They say it depends. Or they shrug. Or they say they have no idea.

Robert said something bad happened at his house. Yes, indeed.

The questioning continued throughout the night, and during all of that time Robert's demeanor was open, his expression of concern apparently genuine, and his manner cooperative. Shown the rusty, twenty-inch World War I bayonet found in the basement, Robert said he had never seen it before.

Robert explained again that after John Jay and his two friends arrived from school he had walked up the stairs to his room to drink beer and watch television. He could smell marijuana coming from his brother's room. After a half hour his brother and friends played Nintendo in the living room, then left. That was it.

For over an hour Wells conducted the questioning himself. He explained the predicament the police had, what with a body in the basement and just the four guys having been present in the house. There had been a time when an interrogation such as this began with a sharp slap across the face. It was as if the suspect needed the punishment to open up. Now if an officer in Nassau County was even accused of such behavior, the district attorney had instructed his assistants that the allegation of police misconduct was to take precedent over the investigation of the crime itself.

But there remained other time-proven techniques. Wells moved in close, violating Robert's body space as he spoke. "Look, I want you to tell me the truth. If you don't want to talk to me just say you don't want to talk to me, but if you lie to me you are going to have big problems."

Wells talked to the young man about society and public mores. He knelt down on one knee after a few minutes and placed his arm across Robert's shoulders. "You've got a problem," he said. "The only way to get a problem solved is to understand you have it. You and I know what happened." He continued in this vein for some time. When that didn't seem to be working he modified his approach.

"What about your brother, John? Could he do this?" he asked.

"No, I don't think so. I really don't think so."

"What about the other guys?"

"No."

Wells appealed to Robert's humanity, to the need to tell them what had really happened, because only then would Robert be unburdened. He described the gruesome condition of the body, the horrible mutilation that the young girl had been subjected to, and pointed out that the other three persons in the house, including his brother, had remained together the entire time. Only Robert had been free to commit the crime.

It was a technique Wells had used with success against even the most hardened cases and was always surprised that it proved so effective. He had concluded that within even a monster was some vestige of humanity.

As Robert responded there was for this one instant a hitch in his voice and Wells believed he detected the slightest moistening of his eyes, but Robert abruptly pulled himself erect, shook his head, and returned to the same monotone reply he had been giving for the last hours.

There is a real person in there, Wells thought. *With luck just maybe we'll reach him yet and end this.* That had been the moment to confront him with his bloody fingerprint. If he had had that he was absolutely convinced a confession would have flooded from the young man. Instead, he turned the questioning over to others.

The interrogators had learned of the latent print at the same time they learned it had been destroyed and knew they were on their own. There was going to be no magic wand to gain a confession. They had to use every device their years of experience had taught them.

Back at the Golubs' home the officers continued with the search. They had now discovered an antique muzzle-loading rifle. On the butt were the familiar reddish-brown stains of blood. It was taken in for examination.

Sharkey had just learned about Harry Finny's story that he had seen John Jay open the door for Kelly. He had already denied placing the call to her. Upstairs Sharkey asked to question the boy again. In the presence of the lawyer and that of his parents, fourteen-year-old John Jay continued to draw strength from his supporters and with each answer was more aggressive and less forthcoming. As one officer observed, "He was king of the castle."

Sharkey asked John Jay to take a lie-detector test. McGoldrick instructed him to refuse, which John Jay did. When Sharkey asked him about letting Kelly into the house, McGoldrick instructed the teenager to stop answering questions.

* * *

Throughout his long, difficult questioning Robert Golub remained collected. He was, he said, as mystified by events as the police and claimed he wished he knew more, but did not. When asked why there was no door to his bedroom, he explained that his father thought he had been borrowing his clothes and in retaliation had removed his door some time before. In only one regard did his story change at all. Initially he insisted that he had last been in the family basement two weeks before when it had been cleaned. Under questioning he had given different time periods, claiming he was remembering trips down the stairs he had not thought of before. Now, he said, he could have been in the basement two days earlier.

So convincing was he that the suspicious officers questioning him wondered among themselves if they had the wrong man. It did not seem possible that they were unable to get anything out of him. They asked if Robert would take a lie-detector test. "Sure," he answered without hesitation.

A polygrapher was summoned and went through the elaborate process of attaching the equipment to his subject. The test lasted for over half an hour. When it was completed the polygrapher informed Wells that the results had been inconclusive. It appeared to him that Robert had intentionally sabotaged the test by moving when he had been cautioned to remain still and by lying on some questions. Certainly the results did nothing to alleviate Wells's suspicions. The officers settled in for another round of questions, questions Robert said he was willing to answer.

Robert had been at the precinct and under interrogation for fifteen hours, almost without letup. At 9:15

Sunday morning, Kelly's fourteenth birthday, Wells received a call from McGoldrick.

"How are you doing?" he asked. "Do you know where Robert Golub is right now?"

"Yes, I do," Wells told him, knowing what was coming. "He's with me.

Instead, McGoldrick said, "Ah, I kind of thought so. We haven't seen him since yesterday."

"No, he's with me."

"Okay, fine. I just wanted to know. Have a nice day."

That, Wells thought, is the strangest call I have ever received from an attorney. Half an hour later his telephone rang again. This time it was an attorney who identified himself as John J. O'Grady. He said that he was now representing Robert Golub and he wanted the questioning of his client stopped. He inquired as to Robert's status.

"He's not under arrest," Wells told him. "If you want, I'll even give him a ride home."

"That's what I want. And no more questions."

Wells went to the interview room and told the officers what had taken place. Not one of them was surprised. The only mystery was why it had taken so long.

Nawrocki had been involved with fingerprint identification for nearly thirty years and had been commander of the Latent Fingerprint Section for ten years. This was an important case and he made the examination of the latent print found on the molding and comparison personally.

First, he observed the reddish-brown markings on the molding that the serologist test performed in the basement told him was blood. Not necessarily human blood, but blood nonetheless. He used magnification of 4.5 power to examine the latent print on the molding in detail. As part of the process to enhance the print, he placed the molding into a sealed box and released Super Glue into it. The fumes from the glue usually caused such imprints to become more visible.

It appeared to him the latent was either a portion of a palmprint, a fingerprint, or possibly even a soleprint from the bottom of a foot. Then for two and a half hours he attempted to match the latent to Robert Golub's fingerprints.

After Nawrocki was finished with his examination he informed Wells of his conclusions. He could not match the latent to Robert. Nawrocki was not especially popular with the homicide detectives. A former paratrooper who still wore a crew cut, he had a precise, inflexible manner of stating his opinion, and once his mind was made up it was nearly impossible to get him to take a second or third look at the evidence. He was the expert and he made that clear.

Wells was thunderstruck upon hearing the news, then became nearly hysterical in his reaction: *Tell me you couldn't read the print, don't tell me it wasn't a match.* The latent print was from the killer. It had to be. Nawrocki was telling him that the print did not match Robert Golub. If it wasn't Robert's, then whose was it?

Six

After arranging for Robert Golub to be taken to his house on Horton Road, Wells drove to his own home where he showered, shaved, and changed clothes. He had not slept in twenty-four hours, but there was no time for that now. This was not the first occasion he had worked such a schedule, nor would it be the last.

He drove to the medical examiner's morgue in Mineola, passing churches filled this sabbath day, and arrived as depressed and deflated as he had ever been in any murder investigation. The previous day's cold rain had turned to snow with the threat of more and the streets were wet. Wells found the day gloomy and depressing.

Autopsies are never pretty and it is no wonder that some religions oppose them or even that families often wish to prevent them. But in the case of murder in the United States, every state requires that an autopsy be performed.

An autopsy is also a key step in any homicide investigation and detectives routinely attend them. Robert Player had agreed to come down to the morgue and make the formal identification of his niece, but was not present for the subsequent autopsy.

Wells began by assisting in the examination of the trace evidence contained in Kelly's clothing, which had been discovered in the attaché cases, and the World War I bayonet removed from the scene. The blade was coated in blood, though most of it was near the hilt and not on the tip. There was no human tissue on it.

The room in which the autopsy was performed had the odor of ripe death. Besides Wells also present were Dr. Thanning, who had pronounced Kelly dead in the Golubs' home; a detective from latent prints; the medical examiner's photographer; Dr. Arlene Colon, a forensic serologist, and Dr. Leslie Lukash, the Chief Medical Examiner for Nassau County. He was also a headstrong, highly experienced medical examiner who was greatly respected by police prosecutors, and the courts. He was, however, not an easy man with whom to work.

Wells observed more than a dozen puncture wounds in the back of the leather bomber jacket Kelly had been wearing that day, puncture wounds that precisely matched the point of the bayonet. It did not take great detective work to conclude that the murderer had confronted Kelly with the weapon, then jabbed her repeatedly as he moved her from the front door through the house and into the basement. The puncture wounds were so pronounced they had lanced through the leather of the jacket, pierced her shirt and penetrated her flesh.

To begin Colon removed all of Kelly's remaining clothing, spread it out on a table then examined it with an ultraviolet light as she searched for semen among other things. She ran the light up and down Kelly's body and in both cases, the clothing and body, found no semen. Colon then took fingernail scrapings which proved negative. Kelly bit her nails and had not retained anything she might have scratched from her assailant under them. Now Colon took both head and pubic hair samples after which the autopsy photographs were taken by the photographer.

Kelly's body was bathed in her own blood. More blood on a body than Wells had ever seen before. Usually human skin would not take a print, but in this situation it was possible. The latent print technician examined every inch of Kelly for a fingerprint. None was found.

Kelly's face and head had been destroyed. The beating about her head alone was violent enough to induce death, violent enough to have caused her death many times over. Lukash stopped counting after he detected two hundred discrete blows to her head. Wells suspected that the killer had used the butt of the antique rifle for most of these blows, but the damage was so extensive it was not possible to match the butt with any individual mark.

Though Kelly's throat had been slit there had also been a determined effort to strangle her as evidenced in part by the knotted bra found with her body. In addition there was a circular hole in her neck that at first appeared inexplicable, until Wells matched the bayonet to it. The indentation coincided with a knob on the handle of the knife. To cause it the murderer would have had to lay the blade across Kelly's throat, then stand with the full weight of his body on the knife, bouncing up and down.

There were signs of trauma over nearly every square inch of her body. She had been beaten everywhere in a frenzy that was virtually incomprehensible. Wells was more convinced than ever that only an incredibly fit and very powerful man could have done this.

And there were the unexplained cuts on her upper

torso. They were not superficial, but they did not extend far into her flesh either. The incisions were long and symmetrical on each side of her body. No one in the room had an explanation for them.

Kelly's vaginal canal and anus had been mutilated in such a manner as to be virtually unrecognizable. The autopsy produced no semen and the damage to her sexual organs was such that it could not be determined if Kelly had been raped. It was not unusual in a sado-sexual murder such as this for no behavior commonly associated with a sexual act to have taken place. The assault and mutilation were the perversion of sexual intercourse and could by themselves be the source of gratification.

Kelly had been laid open from the top of her breast plate—the length of her body—to her anus. An effort had been made to pry her body apart and the effect was to expose her internal organs to view for her killer.

Immediately following the examination for finger-prints and general review of the body, Lukash hosed Kelly's body off so he could examine it for body marks. No swab samples were taken of appropriate areas for signs of rust which would have tied some wounds to the bayonet. And only after Kelly was washed clean did the doctor spot two sets of marks, one on her buttocks in the shape of a half-moon, the other on her neck. They bore some similarity to teeth bites, but it was now too late to swab the areas and obtain sufficient saliva for testing.

A close examination of the numerous wounds con-firmed what Wells had observed in the basement. Many of them, most in fact, were inconsistent with the bayo-net. Some other device had been used. Lukash examined the edges of the wounds by magnification and informed Wells that they held a distinctive "railroad track" pattern which he could not explain. In other words, each cut actually was made by two edges acting in unison, like a pair of railroad tracks. They had not been created by a traditional knife.

When the autopsy was concluded the official verdict was death by asphyxiation due to mechanical trauma and strangulation. For Wells the most disturbing part of the entire exercise was the extent of the bruising. It was massive. So extensive on Kelly's face the traditional purpling had turned black. Dead flesh does not bruise. Kelly had been alive during most of her attack.

The news accounts that Sunday morning were remarkably restrained in reporting the event. The *Daily News* carried the story on page thirteen along with the most recent photograph of Kelly. It reported only that Kelly had ". . . been stabbed several times in the upper body . . ." and that the victim came from ". . . a decent, close-knit family. . . ." *Newsday,* the dominant paper on Long Island, carried an abbreviated story on page nine, lacking even a photograph.

But word of what the officers had uncovered had already spread to the media and a frenzy was building on Horton Road with each passing hour. Reporters were working the street like door-to-door salesmen, interviewing neighbors and children indiscriminately. Horton Road and those living on it were a very hot commodity. Adding to the chaos of the scene, a steady line of curiosity-seekers drove slowly up the street, filing past the Golubs' house.

Wells and his detectives were trying to solve a murder while working in a fishbowl. Nolan watched the gathering of media forces with a premonition that this was just the beginning. He had given this investigation considerable thought and when Wells arrived at the precinct he informed him that Det. George Pierce would be assigned as his partner and as coordinator, a position referred to as the "stooge" by the homicide detectives. Pierce was highly intelligent with a master's degree, of average height with a stocky build. He wore glasses, had graying hair and a ruddy complexion. In describing Pierce the most common word used by his fellow detectives was "honorable."

Nolan had several reasons for selecting Pierce, not the least of which was the officer's steady manner that would serve as a balance to Wells's hotter temperament. He was an excellent detail man and this was a case that was very likely going to hinge on details.

But more importantly, Pierce had recently completed a homicide investigation in which DNA blood testing had been used at the trial to corroborate an otherwise overwhelming case. It had been the first time DNA testing had been admitted in a New York state criminal trial, and Nolan could not shake the judgment forming within him that such experience could prove invaluable here. Until now, no case in the State of New York had ever been solved by DNA tests. Without a break the Kelly Ann Tinyes murder just might be the first.

In addition, the investigation was now formalized with specific officers being assigned certain tasks. McVetty and another juvenile officer were given the job of learning the background of the victim, the names of her friends, her hobbies and social activities. Two homicide detectives were assigned to conduct a similar investigation into the background of Robert Golub and to uncover any other activities "appropriate to the investigation."

By now the press was clamoring for more information as word of the horrors the police were uncovering in the Golubs' basement spread. Neighbors, hearing of them, let themselves think the unthinkable. They did not want to know the details of what had happened to Kelly, but they could not avoid learning them, and with each new revelation they asked themselves. Who could have done this?

Victoria was in a deep state of shock and grief. "It's like a nightmare," she said. "I just wish I could wake up." She had unpacked virtually every photograph of her daughter that she possessed and they were displayed throughout the house, as if somehow the pictures of her daughter could lessen the reality of Kelly's death.

"My baby is dead," Victoria said over and over as she stalked the house in despair. "My baby is dead."

That cold afternoon Richard Tinyes stood in his front yard and spoke to the media. Obviously under stress and barely able to contain his emotions, he read from a short prepared statement thanking, "all the kind people that have made it easier for myself and my wife in this terrible ordeal." He took no questions and returned to his house.

Down the street Elizabeth Golub, in a house filled with detectives, was virtually incommunicative most of the time. Wells had watched her move her mouth as if to speak but no sound had come from her. At times she was nearly comatose as she sat staring off at nothing.

Nolan had been raised in Queens and had spent his career as an officer on Long Island. He had a longtime custom in homicide investigations which he followed in this case. He took Kelly's school photograph and placed it with one of her hideously mutilated body. He put the pair into his wallet where they remained throughout the investigation. From time to time he would remove the photos and remind himself why he and his men were working eighteen-hour days.

Nolan came from a different time, an older generation, when the brutality and violence of the modern era were largely unknown. He had become accustomed to savagery in his years in homicide, but he was no more at ease with it now than when he had been a rookie.

The pervasive presence of reporters and television cameras were turning the neighbors on Horton Road into celebrities and it was already having a damaging impact on the investigation. That day John Jay had been in his second-story bedroom and had waved conspicuously to the reporters, shouting down that he did not know who had killed Kelly. He seemed to love the attention.

While Elizabeth Golub appeared to be nearly in shock from events, Wells had been impressed with John Golub's mature reaction to the investigation. He had extended his fullest cooperation when he could have withheld it or thrown up obstacles. Several times in briefing him as to what was required next, Wells could tell that the father was coming to terms with the reality that at least one of his sons was very likely a killer. The man asked a few pointed questions, but on the whole was tolerating what had to be an unbearable experience with stoic acceptance.

What Wells did not know was that on Saturday, after the questioning was finished and he had been alone,

John Golub had wept for the poor girl found in his basement that day.

Both Earle and Donnell had gone home by now and Wells was briefed in detail about what had finally emerged from their interviews. The picture it gave of the Golub household was disturbing.

Donnell who was fifteen-years-old, had cut his last hour mathematics class at 2:20 P.M. that Friday and instead met with two friends. They suggested the three of them meet later at Carolla's Pizza and from there at 4:30 they would go weight lifting. Shortly after agreeing Donnell spotted John Jay Golub and Chris Earle talking to one of the teachers. John Jay suggested that Donnell join him and Earle, age fourteen, and go to his house. John Jay had three marijuana cigarettes, according to Donnell, that they were planning to smoke there. Donnell agreed to go, but said that he was planning to lift weights later on.

They rode a bus a distance then walked to the Golub residence. As they entered the house they spotted John Jay's older brother, Robert, just inside the front door, sitting on the stairs going through the mail. John Jay asked if there was any mail for him as he was concerned the school had sent a notice to his parents informing them that he had been cutting classes. Robert said there was a letter for their parents from the school and handed it to John Jay for disposal.

The three boys went upstairs to John Jay's bedroom, then followed John Jay into another room, filled with junk. In the middle was a broken bed with a mattress lying on the floor. John Jay displayed a BB gun, then pulled up his shirt to demonstrate his muscles, bragging he lifted weights. He left the room for a minute and turned up the stereo in Robert's room then returned with marijuana. As the boys giggled and behaved as if they did this every day, John Jay lit the joint, drew the smoke into his lungs, then blew it out his nostrils as he passed it around.

Robert came up the stairs from below, stuck his head into the room, looking disoriented and confused. He demanded to know who had turned his stereo on. John Jay said Robert had. Robert appeared to accept that explanation and left.

The three boys smoked a regular cigarette then decided to eat. As they were leaving, Earle stuck his head into Robert's room by moving the sheet aside. No one was there. He saw a vacuum cleaner in the middle of the floor and a chair sitting on top of Robert's bed. John' Jay told him to stay out, that Robert would really get mad if caught him even looking into his room. They walked downstairs to the kitchen on the first floor. It was 3:15 P.M.

Earle called his mother from the kitchen and told her that he would be home around five P.M. Earle opened the freezer and spotted ice pops, but there was a mold of some kind on them and he decided to pass. Donnell located a box of Ritz crackers and the boys ate those. Donnell looked at the clock on the microwave oven and recalled that it read 3:22 P.M. It was time to go.

As they were leaving the house John Jay called out to his brother to tell him he was leaving, but there was no answer. It was hard to hear anything over the stereo. They walked to a nearby elementary school and bullied their way into a ball game with younger children, but lost interest after fifteen or twenty minutes. One of them asked the time and was told it was 3:45 P.M.

The boys left a few minutes later and walked to Carolla's where they ate. After that the boys went to the high school's weight room, but Earle said he didn't want to work out so they split up. Earle and Donnell left together and walked home, each arriving by five P.M. John Jay went to take the bus home and it was at the bus stop just before five P.M. that his father picked him up.

There was one interesting event in the stories. Earle stated that on Saturday, around noon when police officers were in the Golubs' house shortly after Kelly's body had been discovered, he received a telephone call from John Jay. His friend said that if the police asked him questions, Earle was to say nothing about the marijuana. He was to say only that they had played Nintendo in the living room.

Family members confirmed the times as did the telephone company. Neighbors on Horton Road had been interviewed and supported the arrival and departure times for the three boys, adding credibility that they were telling the truth in other areas as well. It was appearing very unlikely any of the three had an opportunity to participate in the murder of Kelly Ann Tinyes.

Wells had begged Nawrocki to attempt another match of the latent print and the detective had begrudgingly agreed. Sunday afternoon Wells received good news when he was informed that the photographs of the print were of exceptional quality. Nawrocki was satisfied he could make a match from them, if a match were possible. Wells's expectations soared once again and he instructed the detectives keeping an eye on Robert to stand alert. As soon as a match was made they were to bring him in for renewed questioning.

Following a brief meeting of investigators at the command van, Wells and Pierce walked down the street to meet with the Tinyes family. Following introductions, Wells informed them that he would be in charge of the investigation and that they should contact him directly with any information or requests. No longer would they be dealing with different detectives. Wells briefed the couple on the status of the investigation, then he and Pierce sat at the kitchen table and Wells wrote out a time log of the events of the previous two days.

Richard Tinyes related how he had been delivering a car and was near his residence in his wrecker when he spotted his daughter and drove her home. He told about her request to go ice-skating and how he instructed her to remain home with her younger brother. When he dropped Kelly off at their house, it was the last time he saw her alive. Victoria had last seen her daughter when she left for school that morning. The parents described their desperate search for their missing daughter, the filing of a missing persons report, then learning that she had been murdered.

Wells spoke with eight-year-old Richie Tinyes but it was apparent that so many people had questioned him, demanded answers of him, that already the events of Friday were slipping from his memory. He said that he received a telephone call at about 3:10 P.M. and the caller asked, "Is Kelly there? This is John." Richie said, "Yes," and called his sister to the telephone. Kelly spoke a short time, the boy thought about two minutes, then Kelly said, "I'm going to Nichol's house," and left. Within five minutes Richie had called his father to report that his sister had left him alone and was sent to find her. On the way to Nichol's house he ran into Sharon Stonel, who told him she had seen Kelly enter the Golub's residence. He described pounding on the door with Harry Finny, calling the house by telephone, but no one was answering, then walking the neighborhood calling out for Kelly over and over.

While the basic structure of the story and most facts were the same as Wells had obtained from the detectives who spoke with the boy on Saturday, he had modified his account, streamlining events. He no longer recalled much of anything beyond what he said in his account, a story it was apparent he had repeated many, many times.

Wells received grudging permission to examine Kelly's bedroom after explaining what he hoped to find. He leafed through her schoolbooks to see any writings or scribblings of boys' names which would suggest she had been involved with someone, or comments by a boy suggesting a special interest in Kelly. He found nothing. Kelly's brush was lying on her dresser and he removed hair samples explaining his need for them and placed the hairs in a plastic evidence pouch.

As he was leaving Richard Tinyes followed him outside. While Victoria had been distraught and under intense emotional pressure, her husband had been stoic and generally uncommunicative since Wells and Pierce had arrived. "Do you want to tell me now what is really going on?" he asked the detectives as if they had been holding something back. Wells assured him that he already had. Richard nodded his head and went back inside.

Wells spoke with John Golub next. It seemed to him he was taking events as well as possible. Visibly upset he had nonetheless extended his cooperation. His manner, his body language, the way he spoke all told Wells that he was prepared to accept that one or both of his sons had murdered Kelly. When one of the Tinyes family glared at him, something that was happening with increasing frequency, he seemed to accept it as a price he was prepared to pay.

At an impromptu press conference on Horton Road, Nolan met with reporters. "We have restricted our entire investigation to that house," he told them. "We are convinced someone in that house is involved in the murder."

The time of the killing had been more accurately fixed at between three P.M. and five P.M. Details of the killing, that Kelly had been stabbed, strangled, and mutilated, were officially released for the first time. The blows to her head alone would have been sufficient to kill her, Nolan reported. He acknowledged that he and his men had more questions of the two Golub brothers, but for now their lawyer had instructed them to stop cooperating.

The intrusion of an attorney so early in the investigation presented Wells and his officers with a serious obstacle. They had many questions they wanted to put to John Jay, but were not allowed to. Though they had questioned Robert for some fifteen hours, officers were still not satisfied with his answers. Wells was certain that if he and his men were given access to the brothers for thorough questioning, this case could be solved within hours. But that option was no longer available.

With all of the evidence and every suspect coming from a single house, one detective suggested to Wells that they were dealing with a "sealed system." A case was going to have to be painstakingly constructed from circumstantial evidence within that system, and in the end there just might not be enough to convict anyone, especially since the key fingerprint had been botched.

Nolan's confirmation that the investigation was so narrowly focused created a stir on Horton Road. The situation was heightened when police sources acknowledged by Sunday afternoon that neither Donnell nor Earle were any longer suspects. They were down to the Golub brothers, and since neither of them was any longer available for questioning, police were focusing on the forensic evidence. Teams of detectives were poring over the house and the basement, and literally hundreds of items had been removed for examination. Even the family bedding had been bundled up and taken away by police. The Golubs were moving elsewhere for a few days.

The investigation was in fact in a quandary. Detectives had learned that of the two brothers, John Jay was the one who exhibited hostile behavior. He was known locally to be a "little crazy." It was John Jay who actually knew Kelly and would have been in a position to lure Kelly into the Golubs' house. Friends reported seeing him and Kelly talking together at the ice rink and around the neighborhood. It occurred to officers that Robert could well be covering for his young brother. If John Jay's two friends were lying about the time he had been out of their sight, then the younger son might be the killer and Robert an accomplice.

On the other hand it took an uncommon amount of force to destroy a face and rip a body apart. If one person had committed this brutal murder alone, the most likely suspect was Robert. Though diminutive, he was a bodybuilder with a powerful physique. Only five feet three inches tall, he weighed one hundred seventy pounds. As a suspect John Jay was right in his aggressive demeanor, but wrong physically; Robert was wrong because of his cooperative, pleasant demeanor, but right physically.

Late Sunday night Nawrocki entered Nolan's office with the results of his final examination. "It isn't Robert's print," he announced firmly.

Nolan could hardly believe what he was hearing. "Are you certain?"

"Yes," Nawrocki said. He had repeatedly compared the photograph print with Robert's and what they had was not a latent print of his fingerprints.

Nolan was staggered. If the print was not Robert's than whose was it? Could it be that Robert Golub might be innocent? He had to consider once again that the killer was the younger brother, John Jay. How could he have been so wrong? All of his experience and intuition said their man was Robert.

He called in Wells to speak to Nawrocki and Wells was equally distraught. He urged Nawrocki to try again, but the businesslike detective refused. He had already checked the latent print against those taken from Robert Golub. The print in the photographs did not belong to him. This was it. There was nothing more to be done.

Seven

Late Sunday night Wells was informed that a six-year-old girl who was a neighbor of the Golubs had information about the murder. Wells and Pierce went down the street and met with her parents They related that their daughter had told them that she had been playing with Sharon Stonel, Harry Finny, and Richie Tinyes on Friday when she saw Kelly enter the Golubs' house.

While the other children banged on the front door of the Golubs' house, the six-year-old had crossed the street, then gone around to look into a basement window. While she was doing that she saw Kelly yelling for help from a second-floor window in the front of the Golubs' house.

Her parents told Wells they believed their daughter and agreed to have her interviewed the next day by a female juvenile officer. Wells didn't know what to think and decided to wait on the results of an interview with the girl.

Wells went home early Monday morning and slept a few hours for the first time since he received word of the discovery of a body in the Golubs'. Back on duty that day he prepared an affidavit which was the basis to obtain a court order directing samples of pubic and scalp hair as well as prints from John Jay, and prints and hair samples from John and Elizabeth Golub. The affidavit stated in part that Kelly Ann Tinyes "was last seen alive at approximately 3:15 P.M.. entering 81 Horton Road, Valley Stream, by neighbors, and that John J. Golub, in contradiction of his story, was the individual who admitted her to 81 Horton Road."

The affidavit went on to place John Jay, Robert, Earle and Donnell in the Golub residence at the approximate time that Kelly was seen entering. Hair found at the scene of the murder did not belong to Kelly so samples were required for comparison.

Most significantly the sworn document stated categorically that the bloody print found in the basement was unidentifiable. It also stated that prints had already been obtained from Robert Golub, Earle, and Donnell and that they had been eliminated as a possible source of the bloody print. The effect of the affidavit was to switch the focus of the investigation to John Jay.

Dr. Lukash, the medical examiner, contacted Dr. Lowell Levine, a Huntington odontologist, recognized as a leading expert in the world in teeth and imprint analysis. He wanted to know if Levine had the available time and was interested in examining the imprints found on Kelly's body that Lukash suspected were bite marks. Levine instructed Lukash to have one-on-one photographs taken and made available to him. Until there was a suspect for comparison, there was nothing more to be done.

* * *

That day two juvenile detectives interviewed the six-year-old girl who claimed to have seen Kelly upstairs in the Golubs' house, screaming for help. She told them the same story her parents had related the previous night, only with new details. She claimed that in addition to seeing Kelly screaming for help from the second-story window, the girl had looked into the basement and witnessed Kelly's murder. In her account, she watched John Jay, Earle, and Donnell dancing around Kelly with knives and having sex with her on a table in the basement. She said that after Kelly was murdered garbage bags had been placed over her feet and head. With child's logic she claimed that Kelly was upstairs screaming for help after the girl said she had seen Kelly murdered in the basement.

The parents confirmed that the family was very close to the Tinyes family and that Richie Tinyes had been staying with them since the discovery of Kelly's body. The first time their daughter had said anything about seeing Kelly had been Sunday night, just before they spoke to Wells.

Sharon Stonel was reinterviewed and said that the girl had been playing in her yard and had never crossed the street. Her mother confirmed the information. No one on the street had seen or heard anyone crying out for help in the Golubs' home. This was supposed to have occurred when the boys were knocking on the door.

The detectives retraced the girl's story and determined that she could not have witnessed the killing from where she said she had been looking into the basement. Finally, the garbage bag had already appeared in the papers and the girl had it wrong. The bag was only over Kelly's feet, not over her head as well.

Learning the details Wells discounted the six-year-old's story as a child's fantasy and let it go. Others on Horton Road would not be so quick to dismiss the account.

On Monday, Earle wanted to change his story and now acknowledge that he, Donnell, and John Jay had not been playing a video game on Friday as he had previously insisted. He admitted the three of them had been smoking marijuana. He was asked to take a polygraph about this and his account of events in general. Donnell was also asked to come down and take one as well. Both boys agreed and passed the tests.

An anonymous source informed Wells that Earle had been telling his friends that Kelly had been murdered by a bayonet. This was information not yet published. Wells questioned the boy who said that when he had been interviewed by the police on Saturday he had overheard two detectives talking about a bayonet. He had been repeating that to his friends.

Since Nawrocki had been unable to match the latent fingerprint to Robert, Earle, or Donnell, Wells had been forced to turn his attention back to John Jay, who on advice of O'Grady was refusing to take a lie-detector test. Even without the test everything Wells understood about this case pointed away from Earle, Donnell, and John Jay. Wells also could not believe the boys were physically capable of inflicting the damage Kelly had suffered.

How was he to accept that three early-teenage boys could murder Kelly, a girl bigger and stronger than any of them, yet not have a drop of blood on their clothing and no damage to their hands? They also played basketball a short time later and no one noticed anything unusual in their appearance. Then after playing basketball the three boys had casually eaten pizza.

Most of all they told the same story again and again, and in the case of Earle and Donnell, had taken and passed a lie-detector test. In addition, Earle was wearing a cast on his hand and a forensic examination had determined no trace of blood and no evidence the cast had been cleaned.

Finally, this had been a sexual mutilation that reflected an advanced state of depravity in the mind of the killer. Wells just could not accept these adolescent boys were of that mind-set.

Yet he was troubled by John Jay and his demeanor. The youth expressed no concern or remorse over the savage murder in his basement of a girl he knew in the neighborhood. From all accounts they had been friendly, even friends. Yet under questioning he had been a smart-ass and generally uncooperative, consistent with someone who had something to hide. He had also been glorying in the attention and the scene of him waving to the press from his second-story bedroom window indicated a callousness toward events that troubled Wells.

But kill Kelly? Wells could not imagine that. Yet someone had done it, and if the latent print did not belong to Robert or John Jay's two friends, than Wells had to take a fresh look at the younger brother.

Though Wells typically solved ninety-nine percent of his murders, for the first time since entering the Golubs' basement, he began to wonder if he was going to be able to bring this one in.

* * *

On Monday, Woodmere Middle School held three assemblies to discuss Kelly's death and to assure the student body that an announcement would be made if an arrest took place. Counselors were on hand and conducted sessions with students throughout the day.

"It's more than curiosity," one of the counselors said. "These kids are terribly shaken. They see Kelly's picture in the paper and on television, and there's still a sense of denial and disbelief. It's different than when a young person dies in a car accident. It's the nature of the assault that shocks the children. There's an air of danger and distrust. Was the person down the block a friend or foe? Those are the kinds of things the kids are asking."

While Roberta and her friends dealt with this tragedy in part with the support of their schoolfriends, the experience for Earle and Donnell at school was very different. As they walked the hallways students moved aside and few chose to talk to either of them.

Nolan gave the press another statement that Monday at the precinct. "We eliminated the two friends after we interviewed them at length," he told reporters officially. "While everyone in this room can obviously feel that someone in that house is responsible for the murder, we do not have sufficient evidence to make an arrest."

One of the supervising detectives also spoke to the press. "Both brothers are suspects," he said, then expressed the frustration he and the others were experiencing. "We have certain people that we've interviewed before and we can't speak to them now. We can't go back and straighten out some things, some questions that we have. It's become very frustrating, where we're going to go with this, I'm not sure at this time. I think the main point of frustration is we have a girl murdered inside of a location that we know, and due to some twists and turns the investigation has taken, including a juvenile and attorneys, it just complicates the case."

Tuesday, John Jay and his parents reported to the precinct as ordered by the court and gave hair samples and fingerprints. At this same time Wells instructed that the thirty-odd officers who had access to the Golubs' house at one time or another during the investigation were also to be printed and to give hair samples. Every possibility had to be accounted for.

The press identified John Jay as the "fourteen-year-old suspect" and that day was the first mention of the extensive mutilation of Kelly that had taken place. The bayonet which had been taken into evidence was publicly identified as belonging to the Golub family.

Wells had a more complete picture of John Jay by this time. He was known as the neighborhood "leech" who hung out with others where he was not welcome and as a teenager with a smart mouth who usually associated with friends a year older than himself. He was also a neighborhood bully who preyed on younger children with obvious relish. Months earlier he had handcuffed a youngster to his garage door as a "joke." The previous Halloween he had so frightened some of the local kids, they had complained and several parents spoke to his father who gave assurances that he would talk to his son about it. John Jay kept knives and a hunting bow and arrow set displayed on the wall in his bedroom. Children claimed he had once shot it through his bedroom door and bragged repeatedly about it.

While both John Jay and Robert denied any knowledge of the bayonet, children in the neighborhood told of visiting with Robert who had brandished the ghastly weapon for them, evidencing a keen fondness for it. Several months earlier John Jay bragged to friends that he had killed a dog with the blade while Robert was rumored to have slain a dog with the bow and arrow.

That night was the first of a two-night wake for Kelly. Roberta debated all day and finally decided to attend the first night which had been reserved for family. A solemn stream of family and very close friends passed into the funeral home to express their condolences, and Roberta stood in line a very long time waiting her turn.

She reached Richard Tinyes first and found him standing under a massive bouquet of white flowers beside the ivory coffin bearing Kelly's body. His daughter's picture, the same one Roberta had seen that morning in the newspaper, was resting on top. Kelly's father was sobbing, unable to speak at all. Roberta told him how very sorry she was. When the girl spotted Kelly's mother she hung back, unable to face the emotional trauma of speaking to her. Finally, she braced herself to say something and forced herself to approach Kelly's mother to express her condolences. Victoria clung fiercely to Roberta and said, "I know how hard you tried to help us. Remember always that Kelly loved you."

* * *

Cotter asked for a meeting of the supervisors working the Tinyes murder as they waited for results of Nawrocki's comparison of the latent print to the prints of the police officers, Earle, Donnell, and the Golubs. There were many issues relating to the investigation he wanted to discuss, not the least of which were police suspicions that his office was responsible for the recurring leaks to the media. The paranoia and doubts were hurting relations between them, and he wanted the police to know that his office was not responsible for them.

While the meeting was in progress they received word that the latent print was not a match to any of those submitted. Wells was so upset he could not remain in the room.

Outside, standing in the hallway, the taste of bile formed in his mouth and he felt as if a hot rod had just been plunged into his gut. He didn't want to have to comprehend the full magnitude of what this meant. Tell him the print belonged to one of the parents, or was a dog print, but don't say they don't know whose print it is. The print matched no one they knew of. How could that be? Now he had a mysterious blood print to contend with.

Wells said later that he felt like going out and slitting his throat. Instead, he went to meet personally with Nawrocki. He explained that he was being told by these results that the fingerprint did not match anyone. He urged Nawrocki to go back and try still one more time. There had to be a match somewhere.

In his abrupt manner Nawrocki explained that the la-

tent print was not a match for any of the prints he had
been given. It was not a match to the Golub parents,
not to John Jay or Robert, neither Earle or Donnell, nor
to any of the police officers who had been in the house
during the investigation. It was pointless for him to pur-
sue this further. He had made his decision and had completed his examination. He was turning the latent print
over to Off. Ronald Crowe for classification and place-
ment into the department's database. That was the end
of it.

Wells's anger and sense of impotence was staggering.
He had little enough faith in proving this case based
upon forensic evidence and Nawrocki's inability to
match the key latent print to any suspect only heightened his sense of futility and frustration.

Birdsall had transported his marked blood samples
from the basement to the department laboratory and had
been running analysis. This was not the ultrasophisti-
cated and incredibly accurate DNA test, but rather the
more traditional tests police departments had been able
to conduct for some years. Performed correctly they
could tell detectives a great deal about who had been
where.

There were ten different types of identifiers, called
PGMs, for which he could test. And if a single specimen
was tested for all ten and their subgroups, he could effectively determine from whom the blood came. While
there had been ample quantities of the victim's blood,
other samples were too sparse to allow such broad
analysis. Since each test consumed a portion of the

blood, Birdsall had to carefully select which identifier for which he would test.

The most blood-consuming test was to classify blood into its general blood type. Every sample of blood he had enough to test came up type O, the most common classification. Blood which came from Kelly was subjected to another identifier and tested as PGM 1+1. He ran more samples of blood and they came up 1+1 as well. Then, on two samples, after hours of work, he tested for the PGM identifier and received a 2+2. These might be type O, like Kelly, but they were not Kelly's blood. One of the samples was on the blue tablecloth, the other on an attaché case.

There were more tests he could run, but he decided not to, not until after he knew the PGMs for those persons who had been in the house. For now, that would have to wait. He told Wells he needed blood samples from the family, then quietly informed him that he thought he had two types of blood. Wells understood the implications at once and told Nolan he required another court order. Two types of blood meant they just might have the killer.

Ronald Crowe, a young and especially sharp officer, had been in the room the last time Wells had begged Nawrocki to take one more look at the latent print. He understood the necessity of making a comparison if it were possible and decided not to simply classify the print Nawrocki had given him, but to try and make a match if possible. Some cases just required more effort than others.

To overstep your supervisor is something not many

officers in Crowe's place would have done, but it was in his nature to do whatever was necessary to solve a case. In a previous murder investigation he had personally checked fifteen thousand sets of fingerprints before making a match.

The first matter that Crowe considered was that the fingerprint, if that's what it was, had been made in blood. Crowe had worked a previous case in which a print had been left in blood and what he recalled was that it had been unlike the normal latent print. A print made from blood was not formed by the ridges as in a typical latent print, but from the valleys between the ridges. This gave it a very different look.

From the time he received the print and continuing all day Monday, Crowe compared the photograph to Robert's prints. As if he were working the photograph like a piece in a jigsaw puzzle, he tried it over and over again across every portion of the prints that had been taken from Robert on Saturday.

Nawrocki had been correct, Crowe at last concluded. The print was not a latent fingerprint of Robert Golub. It was not a finger print at all.

On Tuesday, Crowe went to Wells. "Look at this," he said, placing Robert's prints on Wells's desk. Then he brought out the photograph of the bloody impression taken from the basement. He carefully slid it away from the fingertips to the portion of the hand between the thumb and forefinger, on the edge of the palm. "Use this," he urged, handing Wells the magnifying glass.

Wells leaned down and stared. It took a moment for his eyes to register, then there it was. A perfect match. He looked up with a grin. It was a fold print of the portion of the skin between the thumb and first finger.

They had him. It had been Robert Golub who had left his bloody print at the scene of the murder.

"I've matched twelve points," Crowe told him. This was more than what was required for a legal determination. Crowe was deservedly pleased with his success.

Then, with a sinking heart, Wells recalled the affidavit he had filed the previous day. He had stated categorically that the latent print did not match Robert Golub. There was going to be hell to pay for this. He thanked Crowe, but knew he would have to go to Nolan to explain one more strategic error in dealing with the forensic evidence.

Eight

Wells knew he would take heat over Nawrocki's inability to properly match the latent print. He went first to Cotter to tell him the good news before informing Nolan what had happened. There was time enough to consider the consequences of the affidavit later. For now he wanted to bask in the pleasure of success.

But before Wells got to Nolan Nawrocki went to the lieutenant himself. He had been the one to report the print could not be matched. Now one of his men had succeeded. He had delivered the bad news, it was his place to bring the good.

"John," he said, "we were successful in identifying Robert Golub's palmprint as the one."

Nolan could hardly believe what he was hearing and could not contain himself. He shot out of his chair, ran around the desk, and kissed Nawrocki on the forehead.

He took Nawrocki with him and had the ex-paratrooper inform the chief of detectives that his team had successfully matched the latent print. The case was back on track, Nolan told his boss. It was all going to work out after all.

The next day at a meeting with Wells and the supervisors on the case, Cotter explained that they must get corroboration of the match. Nawrocki had insisted the latent print did not compare with any of the samples and they should expect the defense to call him as a witness. Wells had submitted an affidavit to the court stating that the latent did not come from Robert Golub. Now they had a technician, a subordinate to Nawrocki and presumably less skilled, who said he had a match. What they would have was one department expert testifying contrary to another. No, they would need an outside expert opinion.

The police officers were offended at the suggestion. After all, hadn't they worked this out within the department? There was no greater insult to an investigation than to have to draw on outside assistance, to acknowledge your own inadequacies in areas of traditional law enforcement.

Cotter said this was essential and was a prosecutorial decision. He left later that day with Crowe for the FBI forensic evidence facility in Washington, D.C. The pair met with the FBI's foremost print expert who soon made twenty-one matches of points on the print to Robert Golub. There was absolutely no question the latent was his.

Wells's satisfaction was tempered by what he knew was coming. When word leaked to the press, as Wells knew it must, it would be difficult to explain to the public why they did not simply arrest Robert Golub. It would be difficult to explain to the public the fact that the basement where the print had been located was in Robert's own house. What was unreasonable about a print of his being there? Robert had given different versions of when he had last been in that basement, but his final account placed him there two days before the murder. He could claim he had cut his hand then. There was no way to establish the print had been left only by the murderer at the time of the killing. It was a powerful bit of evidence, but it was not enough to charge Robert Golub with murder or to arrest him.

Wells understood that. He doubted the reporters or public would.

On Wednesday, the funeral service for Kelly was held at St. Joseph's Roman Catholic Church in Valley Stream. Roberta, who was Jewish, had never been inside a church before. It was so filled that many attending were forced to stand lining the walls. It was a closed casket ceremony, but Richard Tinyes had ordered the coffin opened in private for him earlier and he had looked for a time on the destroyed body of his firstborn child. What he saw may explain what was to come.

Roberta and her three friends who had been closest to Kelly had been asked by the school to write something in memory of their friend. It had been read over the PA system at school for those who would not be attending the funeral and to her surprise the priest read it as well:

Dear Kelly,
    Sometimes the hardest word to say is good-bye. . . . You were a very caring, feeling and emotional person. You were special. We remember the way you always moved your hair to the side . . . we remember you waving to your friends through classroom doors . . . we wanted you to remember your fourteenth birthday with happiness. You were

the prettiest, most delightful friend. We love you, Kel. We'll miss you. Goodbye from all of us.

At St. Charles cemetery Kelly was buried before a gathered throng of one thousand. Television cameras and newspaper photographers were everywhere, turning the tragedy into a circus for public consumption.

Afterward, those closest to Kelly were still numbed by their grief, but slowly they and the neighbors on Horton Road began thinking more clearly about what had taken place. It was true, they learned, that John Jay and Kelly knew one another. Neighbors told of seeing them speaking, standing with others on the sidewalk. Wells had located one witness who claimed he had seen Kelly and John Jay walking down Horton Road holding hands. They had not been anything more than casual neighborhood friends, but even that came as a surprise to the Tinyes family.

John Golub had done his cause in the neighborhood little good when he told the family lawyer to instruct his sons to stop cooperating with police. He made matters worse on Saturday, one week after Kelly's body was discovered in his basement, when he told a reporter that his sons were innocent and that he was worried about people's reactions toward them and his family. "I'm afraid that someone's going to overreact . . . I've heard people refer to this as a 'death house,' " he said. He told the reporter that he suspected someone had snuck into his basement to commit the murder.

Wells had experienced difficulty reading John Golub from the beginning. He was not a man easy to get close to. Still, from the first, the father had seemed to Wells to accept that one of his sons had murdered Kelly. Before the search warrant was issued he had allowed the police to remain in his house. He had not defended Robert to Wells, rather he had asked significant questions to assure himself that someone else could not possibly have done it.

But when Wells filed his affidavit with the court earlier that week and stated under oath that the print in the basement did not match Robert, John Golub's demeanor underwent a profound change. Suddenly he behaved as if his son were innocent and had begun to argue that someone had snuck into the basement and murdered "that girl," as he called Kelly. When word of the match to Robert appeared in the press, John Golub appeared disbelieving, as if the evidence had been manufactured. No longer, it appeared to Wells, did he seem to trust the police.

From the moment the body had been discovered, the local media, in particular *Newsday,* had covered the story extensively. The brutal murder of Kelly Ann Tinyes, a white girl from a respectable family in quiet Valley Stream, was "newsworthy."

Newsday's reporters dogged the investigators relentlessly and printed information about the investigation before Nolan was ready to go public with it. The reporters had hounded neighbors and gone to the teenage hangouts to obtain statements. Donnell and Earle had been interviewed by a reporter at Carolla's where they casually shared their statements to the police. An article appeared every day in *Newsday* from the date of the murder for thirteen consecutive days, with more than one article in some editions.

The reporters were giving the detectives no room in which to conduct their investigation. Each morning Wells held his briefing for his three teams of investigators, learned what they had discovered and gave that day's assignments. He was informed that a newspaper reporter was leaning up against the van with her ear to the side listening in on his briefings. He explained to the reporter his need for at least some privacy and that these briefings were confidential. He and his men were working eighteen-hour days and they could use a little consideration.

She asked aggressively if he had ever heard of freedom of the press and the people's right to know? She told him the sidewalk was public property and if she chose to lean against the van she had every right to. Wells believed the press coverage to date had been largely negative concerning the police and he didn't want to give one more reporter a reason to write more nasty articles so he backed off. But starting the next day the daily briefings were held in secret at a diner in a nearby town.

Despite the sensational reporting of a sensational murder, the paper was generally accurate in its coverage and proved week after week that its sources were intimately familiar with the investigation. It was apparent to Wells by now that someone on the investigative team was leaking information. He knew every one of the officers personally and was certain none of them would do something so despicable, but someone he trusted was.

Nolan was equally concerned about the leaks. Almost as quickly as Wells gathered a new fact, it appeared on television or in the newspaper. The detectives had no room in which to work, no time to sort out the meaning of the clues. Nolan also knew his men eyed with distrust his chummy relationship with the media. Nolan's role was to contain the media, if possible, to limit the release of information, if possible, so as not to hinder or imperil the investigation. The problem he was having was that it was not always possible to control the information. A dozen officers or more had access to it and a leak could occur at any point.

Nolan gathered the Homicide Squad and cautioned them not to leak any information about the investigation. It would do no good and could cause a great deal of harm. The men looked at one another suspiciously but each day thereafter confidential information continued to be printed in the press. The ability of the team to work together as a cohesive unit was threatened.

It was like a millstone around the neck of the investigation, Nolan thought. Men were reluctant to work with one another or to share information. It was intolerable, but there was nothing more to be done about it.

From the pages of their daily newspapers and by rumor, the families on Horton Road came to learn the dark secrets of the Golubs. Every family has matters which are kept within the household, but in the Golubs' case their lives fed the local rumor mills. The comparison of life behind the walls of the house was as striking as the difference between its neat outward appearance and the grubby clutter of the interior.

Wells had formed his own impressions of the family from what he had observed inside the Golubs' house. Elizabeth Golub was a collector of miscellaneous items to a degree he had not imagined existed. In her bedroom he had found new men's suits packed together in a closet so tight it had not been possible for him to slip his hand between them.

Wells did not accept Robert's explanation for having no door to his bedroom. It was not normal to hang a sheet there instead, and a father would not do something like that because his son was borrowing his shirts. No, there was more to it. Perhaps it had been a way to limit Robert's use of drugs in his bedroom. Or perhaps Robert had sexual practices the father was trying to inhibit. Wells didn't know.

But as unsettling as details of the housekeeping had been for the neighborhood to learn, more disturbing was the nature of the family. The tabloid ran a series of articles reporting that the Golub family ate its meals singularly, sequestered in their dingy bedrooms, that Robert's bedroom door had been permanently removed by his father, and that Robert and John Jay both used drugs regularly.

Some ten days after the murder, Wells believed they had resolved the dilemma over what weapon had been used to cut Kelly. The bayonet had clearly done the grossest butchery, but much of the cutting had been performed by another instrument. Exactly what it was had puzzled Wells for days. They had tested every possible knife in the household for traces of blood or a matching cutting edge, all without success.

Found inside one of the attaché cases had been a blood-soaked tablecloth. It was different from the other articles of bloody material because when Wells laid it out, he noticed that the stains appeared to match when the cloth was folded on itself, much like folding a Rorschach test in half. Each time he folded the material the stains continued matching until the tablecloth was the size of a small handkerchief. That was its shape when it had become bloody.

There are slices all the way through the cloth consistent with the folding, slices that matched the small cuts on Robert's hand. Birdsall called Wells's attention to the piece of glass he had located near the box of cases, glass that had been covered in blood. Wells compared the glass to the tablecloth and concluded that Robert had held a piece of broken glass with the tablecloth to shelter his hand and performed most of the cutting on Kelly's body with this crude instrument.

A piece of glass had two cutting edges and in this case they precisely matched the "railroad" track pattern the medical examiner had observed and been unable to explain at the autopsy. It also appeared that the killer had pressed so hard the glass had sliced through the folds of material and cut into his own hand. The very idea was ghastly.

John Golub had not missed the mark when he complained that his neighbors were calling his home a "death house." A steady stream of gawking strangers drove up Horton Road, pointing out the Golubs' house as though it were displayed in a freak show. Small children dared one another to sneak closest to its walls. Neighbors were seen standing on the sidewalk or in their yards staring at the house for protracted periods, as if by looking they could somehow come to terms with the enormity of what had taken place there.

John Jay was portrayed in the press as a habitual truant who, along with his friends, bullied neighborhood children. When he and his companions went to play basketball the day of the killing, it had not been a friendly neighborhood pickup game. John Jay and his friends were clearly stoned and were aggressive with the other players. When they left John Jay told them to tell no one they had seen him and his friends, or he would come back and bust his knuckles on them. Such conduct on the day of the murder only heightened suspicion toward him.

If neighbors were concerned over John Jay what they were learning about Robert proved deeply disturbing. Since graduating from high school he had made almost no new friends. He held a job as a deliveryman for a time but received so many tickets his driver's license was pulled, and the previous summer he had been fired.

Robert was sensitive about his size. While still in high school Robert had started working out in a corner of a nearby gym called the midget corner with other diminutive teenagers, adding bulk to a body that would never be tall. He used steroids to help the process and was what one of the bodybuilders commonly referred to as a "juice addict." His three-hour workouts were a daily release for him, something one of his friends told officers Robert required to ease "stress." He would not elaborate.

But since losing his job Robert had been unable to afford the gym and had lain about his parents' house, reading muscle magazines, piles of graphic pornography, and ingesting his daily supply of steroids. Both needles and drugs had been discovered in his bedroom.

Despite his seemingly placid exterior Robert was known to have a violent temper. In December 1987 he had competed in a local amateur bodybuilding contest and had placed fifth out of sixth. He became furious when told and smashed the proffered trophy, then refused to take the stage with the other contestants for the presentation to the winner. As a consequence he had been barred from further competition.

Though his father could use his help at the family service station, Robert was fastidious in his appearance and refused any work that soiled his hands. All this was in sharp contrast to the soft-spoken young recluse the neighbors knew.

Detectives interviewed a former friend of Robert's who painted a disturbing picture of the young man. He had known Robert for the last year and had become a close friend. He confirmed Robert's drug use, stating that the two often smoked marijuana together and for a period used crack cocaine regularly. In addition to the frequent use of drugs, Robert also drank up to two six-packs of beer a day.

Though he was not himself a bodybuilder the friend often went with Robert to Whitehall's Gym in Lynbrook and watched him work out. There Robert told him that steroids were important to help his body development, and he had shown his friend a bottle of pills he said were steroids, which he routinely took. He also displayed a bottle of liquid steroids and the syringe with which he injected himself. The friend had grown tired of all the drug use and by the end of the year had broken himself away from what he viewed as Robert's unwholesome influence.

Wells was not surprised by what he learned. In his

opinion Robert was a loser with a Napoleonic complex, living a dead-end existence, mooching off his parents while his friends from high school had gone on to college and jobs. He had lost both his driver's license and his job. He spent his days sleeping, lifting weights—and using drugs.

What Wells could not calculate was the role steroids had played in the murder. He knew the phrase " 'roid rage," but Robert had not been tested in the hours after the murder and there was no way to determine if he had been using steroids when Kelly had been killed. He knew that some regular abusers of steroids complained of a diminished sex drive, but he had also heard that users claimed that steroids heightened not just their anger and aggression, but bragged it increased their sexual appetite as well. Unless Robert was willing to discuss it, however, Wells doubted he would ever understand the role steroids had played in this murder.

In addition to pornographic magazines detectives had discovered in Robert's room, a graphically violent pornographic videotape of a cheap film made during the 1950s. Wells along with Nolan and other homicide detectives had watched the movie back at the squad. In it a naked woman is having intercourse with a drug dealer and is caught in the act by her boyfriend. She goes into the bathroom and then stumbles out a moment later covered in blood. She falls and dies and the film ends.

In an attempt to ease neighborhood tension and concerns that a killer was on the loose while the investigation proceeded, two-officer walking patrols were assigned to Horton Road. In addition, radio cars were constantly in the immediate neighborhood ready to respond on a moment's notice. Officers were also placed, with the permission of the owners, in strategic backyards so that every part of Horton Road was under scrutiny.

Wells had by now gathered a substantial amount of forensic evidence, though what it meant had to wait on laboratory analysis. Altogether more than four hundred items had been collected, and 231 photographs had been taken. Officers had pulled the drains from every sink, bath, and shower in the house to test for blood. They had extracted the sump pump and hose drainpipe from the Golubs' washing machine in case the clothes the killer had worn had been washed. They had gathered buttons, broken glass, doorknobs, plastic bags, metal scale, paper, cloth, more items than could be easily listed.

Detectives had vacuumed Robert's bedding once it was taken in for examination and found one strand of a woman's hair. In addition, pubic hair which was not Kelly's had been found on her body. They had more than one hundred samples of blood, and to assist in determining whose it was the entire Golub family was required twelve days after the murder to give blood samples to the police by court order as Wells had requested.

Five forensic technicians were laboring over the items taken from the Golubs' home. They were acutely aware that a single hair follicle or a drop of blood could make or break the troubling case.

Birdsall had dropped all his other cases and was now

working on this one exclusively. In a small room at the Nassau County Police Department, he was working eighteen-hour days conducting hundreds of tests on the blood samples which had been lifted from the basement. In a typical murder investigation he would have been expected to perform perhaps three tests then leave it at that.

As was the case with all the technicians, Birdsall had been a police detective before specializing in forensic evidence and he approached his tasks with the mind of a skilled investigator. With blood samples from those living in the house, he worked backward toward the samples he had taken at the murder scene.

John Golub, his sons Robert and John Jay, were all type O. Elizabeth Golub was type B, and Birdsall eliminated her at once. He had run the PGM test on the other blood and John Golub tested as 1+2, so he was also eliminated. Both Robert and John Jay, however, tested as PGM 2+2. So the second blood samples he had found in the basement could belong to either of the brothers.

But there was another test Birdsall could perform, a subgroup of the PGM test, known as the genetic marker, or EAP. There were six of these subgroups. He ran the test against the samples drawn from the family. Kelly's EAP he knew was A. John Golub's was BA, and Elizabeth Golub tested as BC. John Jay was a B and Robert tested a CA.

Now that Birdsall knew what he was looking for, he went to the blood samples he had collected in the basement, in particular to the two that had tested with PGMs of 2+2. Both samples tested the same: CA. In all it had

taken twenty-one individual tests before he had reached
this finding. He took his results to Steinbeck.

* * *

Steinbeck prepared a map of the basement and on it
marked the location of every specimen of blood, tissue,
hair, and other evidence his men had gathered and
tested. The map was as detailed as a scale model of a
battlefield. Only then was he ready to meet with Nolan,
Wells, and Cotter.

The men were told for the first time that tests revealed the presence of blood from only two sources:
Kelly Ann Tinyes and Robert Golub. No other blood
had been found in the basement. While Birdsall could
not testify for a fact the blood came from Kelly and
Robert, he had established it to date with a likelihood
of 1 in 400. More tests could very well raise that figure.

Most significantly from a prosecution point of view,
the tests he had run eliminated without a doubt every
other person known to have access to the Golubs' house
at the time Kelly had been murdered.

Wells had hoped that the nicks on Robert's hands
meant he had left some blood at the murder site, but
with all the blood from Kelly he had not been optimistic
Birdsall would locate any, or that it would be enough
for testing. But this development along with the palmprint was enough for Wells as it was for Nolan, and
they were prepared to make an immediate arrest. The
pressure from the media and from command in the police department had become monumental. Surely this
was sufficient.

But Cotter was not so certain. There had already been
one mistake with the palmprint and he wanted to

strengthen his case in every regard possible. Cotter told Steinbeck that samples of the blood were to be sent for the far more sophisticated process of DNA coding. He was not going to lose this case because a defense attorney successfully convinced a jury the investigation had been sloppy.

It had only been during the last few months that either Nolan or Wells had even heard of DNA testing. Wells thought it was just a variation of the serology tests officers routinely performed, and Nolan knew it had just started making its appearance in criminal trials. Cotter demonstrated a lot of confidence in it and that was good enough for him.

Nolan checked with the police department administrators and was shocked when they refused the five thousand dollars the DNA tests were likely to cost. The budget, they said, couldn't handle it. Nolan was angry at the parsimonious attitude. Wells and his team had already worked hundreds of hours in overtime on this case and no one had told him to put a stop to it. This few thousand dollars was nothing compared to what the total cost of this case was certain to be before it was finished, but by refusing to spend it they jeopardized the conviction. He told his senior officers that, but they were unpersuaded. There would be no DNA tests.

Nine

Amid mounting public pressure and a neighborhood on the verge of panic, press reports announced the police had decided who had murdered Kelly Ann Tinyes. Responding to leaks, Nolan was forced to acknowledge to reporters they felt they had enough evidence to make an arrest though for the time being no arrest would be made. His frustration with whoever was leaking information heightened since it only served to increase the pressure on his men.

The pressure on Nolan from the chief of detectives and others in command had become relentless. He was required to attend meeting after meeting, listening to endless speculation, second-guessing, and wild theories as to how the investigation ought to proceed. One senior official had told Nolan that when he saw John Golub's Rolls-Royce parked in his driveway, he was certain that it held the key to the murder. More than once Nolan had taken Wells aside and told him to remember that "Success has many fathers, failure is an orphan."

Wells knew what Nolan meant. He had felt like an orphan since the first days of this investigation, and increasingly he and Nolan were standing alone against the unbelievable pressure from all sides. In response Nolan felt it necessary to hold a daily meeting with Wells and the detectives working the murder so he could be briefed on every detail. The effect of passing this information up the chain of command only increased idle speculation and heighten the pressure put on Nolan, Wells, and the investigation in general.

Increasingly, Nolan appeared depressed. His usual pale Celtic complexion was often florid, and the photographs of him in newspapers, along with his frequent appearance on television, revealed a grim countenance. Wells wondered how any of them could continue to hold up with so much bearing down on them.

Nolan and Wells informed Cotter that the DNA tests were out, expecting another strong reaction. Instead, Cotter said he had feared as much and had done some checking. He told them if that was the decision, then his office would pay for the tests. Pierce had previous experience with Lifecodes, then located in upstate New York, and with Lorah McNally, the laboratory supervisor. Lifecodes was the foremost DNA lab in the nation and he strongly recommended they use the company.

The next day, Wednesday, March 15, the three men and Birdsall drove to Valhalla, New York, to meet with McNally, who had not previously heard of the case. They presented to her the two attaché cases and five other blood samples they wanted tested. The smear was so faint on one of the cases that Birdsall had to hold it to the light before she could see the fine film. She told them she understood their desire for speed, but results would take weeks, if not longer.

Cotter told an increasingly anxious Nolan and Wells that it was his decision to wait on an arrest until the following Wednesday, two and a half weeks after the body was discovered, when he could present the case to a grand jury. The newspapers suggested there was a raging controversy in the investigation that raised public concern about its competence. In the meantime the two Golub brothers were still publicly identified as the only suspects.

For once the press was underplaying a major story, for behind the scenes there was violent disagreement over how to proceed. For days there had been considerable argument about what details of the investigation should be made public. Nolan tried to explain to the District Attorney's Office that he was having little success in limiting knowledge of the investigation since the press was having no difficulty obtaining its information elsewhere. Everyone was feeling the heat. Wells had snapped at superiors at the police department. Tempers were often short in meetings between Nolan and Wells and the District Attorney's Office. An ill will set in that lingered for years afterward.

During an especially frustrating period a complaint from the D.A.'s office about the investigators working the case being "assholes" made its way to Wells, who traded some heated words with his colleagues there. Pierce made a point of explaining the anger and frustration all the detectives were experiencing during the investigation. Everyone was snapping at everyone else and such remarks only made the situation worse. They needed to work together to get this job done.

Wells, supported by Nolan, insisted on making an immediate arrest, but Cotter vehemently disagreed. The officers argued that as long as Robert Golub was free another young girl could be in danger, and there was no guarantee that Robert might not suddenly flee their jurisdiction.

In addition, given the mood on Horton Road, the detectives could not rule out the possibility of vigilante justice. How long could the police expect the neighborhood, in this current climate, to behave in a civilized manner? The newspapers were reporting the police had enough evidence to make an arrest and Nolan had been forced to admit it. If they refused to proceed it made them appear at the least uncaring, at worst incompetent. The pressure on neighbors to act on their own might prove more than hotheads could withstand. Wells informed Cotter that Robert was under surveillance and he was prepared to order a summary arrest.

Cotter said he understood the detectives' concerns and, in fact, agreed with them, but then explained why that could not happen. If Wells and his men made an arrest at once, the prosecutor would be compelled to present the evidence he had at a preliminary hearing where the defense attorney could attack its credibility. The more detailed DNA laboratory analysis of the blood samples was still under way and until it was back the district attorney did not want to be making his evidence public or subject to court inspection. Instead, the prosecutor wanted to present the circumstantial case to a grand jury where there would be no cross-examination of his witnesses, no meaningful scrutiny of the blood samples and police analysis. That meant taking the risk of leaving the suspect on the streets a few days longer.

Nolan didn't like it and Wells hated the decision even more, but they had no choice but to agree to hold off on making an arrest. God help them all if something happened in the meanwhile, to which Cotter could only add "Amen."

Though the Golubs' house was about to be released back to the family, the police van remained stationed outside on the street, in the hope that new witnesses would come forward and to maintain a visible police presence in a volatile situation. The van had been the subject of at least one press account, one Wells resented deeply, in which he and his men were described as aliens descending on the otherwise peaceful neighborhood. Here he and his detectives were working around the clock to bring a killer to justice and they had to stand for reporters calling their presence at a crime scene "alien." He had no appreciation of the job reporters were doing in this case.

John Golub returned every day or so to check on the condition of his house and to pick up items his family needed, but for nearly two weeks the Golubs lived elsewhere, and the rest of the family had not been seen on Horton Road.

The father's visits to his house were a constant source of neighborhood agitation. The neighbors would call Wells and demand a meeting with him. He would rush over to Horton Road and attempt to calm everyone down. They were not sympathetic when he explained that John Golub had the right to go to his own house. It was clear to Wells that they wanted the man, and the family, banished from the neighborhood.

By this time fear was pervasive on the once quiet street, and grandparents asked that grandchildren not come to visit for the time being. Other neighbors were focused on who had committed the murder and what that said about his family. One fifteen-year-old commented, "My sister in college told me the first three months of a baby's life determines how it's going to be—though I still think it's possible somebody can be born evil."

Some neighbors had made their feelings toward the Golubs known as rumors flew that the family was planning to move back into their house. "I don't think they would be welcome back here," one said. "I can't see how they could come back after this."

Wells could easily understand the neighborhood's frustration with the police department. Though he was occupied every waking hour with the excruciating details of the murder investigation, he could still see the problem from the public's point of view.

A body of a young girl had been found in the basement of a house. Her time of death had been fixed to a period when four individuals had been present. Two of these, friends of one who lived in the house, had been ruled out as suspects. If you have a body and two suspects, what could possibly be the problem with making an arrest? Aren't the police competent enough to figure this out? Didn't the police care about the safety of the community, even more importantly, the safety of the families living on Horton Road?

Wells understood perfectly. What he knew the neighborhood did not appreciate was his own frustration. He had pulled Kelly Ann Tinyes from that closet and examined her shattered body in detail. He, of all people, knew the pain she had experienced, the terror she endured as the assault continued on her. He had seen the sheer brutality and savageness of her wounds. Then, knowing all of this, he had been forced to leave that house without solving the case and to work relentlessly for over two weeks before he could even consider making an arrest.

Almost every day Wells and Pierce met with the Tinyes family to deliver a progress report. Even though someone connected to the family had leaked details that he had asked not be made public to the press, Wells still felt an obligation to keep them apprised of what he knew. He had failed to solve at least one murder because the victim's family had become alienated from him early in the investigation and he was not about to let that happen here.

These meetings routinely lasted two to three hours and almost without exception the family insisted that Wells take some action to prevent the Golubs from returning to their house. The Tinyeses were also pressing for an immediate arrest, but that decision had been made by others. After nearly every meeting Richard Tinyes followed the detectives out into his yard.

"So tell me what is really going on," he would ask. Wells explained he had already done that, but Richard's manner said he did not believe him.

It was apparent by this time that the Tinyes family was of the firm opinion that the entire Golub family was implicated in their daughter's murder. Wells could understand these sentiments, but he explained that wasn't the way the law worked. But no one seemed all that interested in Wells's explanations.

Wells watched with apprehension the tension on Horton Road grow. He wished the reporters and television

crews would go home and give the neighborhood som
time to cool off. Instead, every hour he was seeing mor
and more of them on Horton Road. He wished th
neighbors and the Tinyeses would forget about th
Golubs even as he knew that was not possible. He coul
tell this case was building toward something. There wa
the sense that another shoe was about to drop.

As Nolan expected, the neighbors on Horton Roa
demanded to know of him why no arrest was bein
made when the newspapers said the police knew wh
the killer or killers were. Nolan could make no publi
statement that responded adequately to them and his re
fusal to give a satisfactory answer was like tossing gaso
line onto a fire. He knew it, but had no alternative.

Tension on Horton Road mounted until on Saturday
March 18, the Golubs drove up to their house early i
the evening. Wells had just released the house back t
them with the expiration of his search warrant. It wa:
bad enough that John and Elizabeth Golub had com
back. Unfortunately, they brought their two sons wit
them.

The Tinyeses and Players along with other neighbor:
established a vigil on the Golubs' house, at first stand
ing quietly across the street.

The timing could not have been worse. Word ha
spread earlier that day that Wells had interviewed a six-
year-old neighborhood girl who claimed she had witnessed Kelly's murder and that everyone in the house
including the parents, had danced around Kelly's body

brandishing knives. The story Wells had heard nearly two weeks earlier had finally surfaced with even more embellishment.

For some days now there had been a tendency to talk about "that house," as though the house itself were evil, and "those people," as if everyone in the Golub family shared responsibility. The little girl's story was more of the same and whipped neighborhood opinion into a frenzy.

Word of the Golubs' return spread quickly and reaction by neighbors was nearly tribal in nature, primeval in its origin. Neighbors questioned how it was possible for "those people" to sleep in that house knowing what had taken place.

By morning the numbers standing watch grew as well-dressed neighbors drifted down the street to see what was taking place, then joined the crowd that by now had moved to the sidewalk directly in front of the Golubs' house. At midmorning more than seventy-five people stood there murmuring their disapproval, glaring at the shuttered windows.

In less civilized times there might have been a house burning, perhaps a lynching, or the crowd might have beaten the Golubs, then banished them from the community. But these were days of criminal laws, of courts and trials.

Now sixteen days after the murder of Kelly Ann Tinyes, Robert Golub left his house at 11:30 A.M. and began a brisk walk to the nearby King Kullen. He was immediately followed by more than four dozen people who believed he was a killer. Robert was walking quickly along the sidewalk, his steps lengthening, almost as if he were about to sprint. Dogging his every step along with the pack were television cameras, filming as if this were a scene in a motion picture.

As Robert approached the neighborhood King Kullen Supermarket, he no longer held himself back and suddenly broke into a run. The pursuing crowd, immediately energized, leaped after him, clinging to his heels, pressing down on him. He ran faster until just a second ahead of the mob he bolted into the store, slamming the doors open, spinning on his heel, staring back through the glass.

His chest heaved and the sounds of his breathing could be heard across the room. He stared at the people, many of whom he had known his entire life, though the look in their eyes as they watched him said he was someone they had never known at all.

Slowly, with just a handful at first, a chant began. It grew in force and with rapid unison. The cameras circled the mob, angling for the best shot. The faces of the people contorted in rage, fists shaking the air as they shouted, over and over, "Dev-il, Dev-il! Dev-il!"

Inside the store Robert backed from the doorway as if the chant were a physical assault. He licked his lips then cast his eyes quickly side to side as if searching for a means of escape or perhaps for someone to help him.

Outside the crowd chanted, louder and louder. The camera crews were maneuvering to get a shot of him through the window when, after a few moments, three men in the crowd moved to enter the store. Robert Player pushed the doors open, glared at Robert Golub, then with his two companions crossed the few steps and stood confronting him.

Robert swallowed hard, his eyes searching the faces of each of them before him in turn, then he asked, "Do I know you?"

After a moment Player, who was standing closest to him, said, "No, but I know you."

The young man took in each of the men again in quick order, then suddenly blurted, "I'm innocent. I didn't do it!"

His accusers said nothing while outside the store the crowd chanted, "Dev-il! Dev-il! Dev-il! Dev-il!"

The plainclothes police officer who had Robert under surveillance had followed Robert down the street, had entered the King Kullen, and now stood between Robert and the three men confronting him. He was certain that if he didn't put a stop to this someone was going to kill Robert Golub.

The officer pulled Robert into a storage area. "Are you crazy, or what?" he screamed at Robert. The detective told the manager to call for backup. Outside the crowd was increasing in anger.

When the uniformed officers arrived they provided security and escorted Robert Golub out the back door where he climbed into a waiting car driven by his older sister. The crowd realized what was taking place and ran to the rear of the building where police attempted to hold them back without effect. Television camera crews shoved their cameras into the faces of the Golubs and ignored police efforts to hold them at a distance.

As the car lurched forward, stalled, then lurched again, neighbors spat on it, then pounded on the hood and roof with their fists. The car pulled free of the crowd and the neighbors sprinted behind it in hot pursuit down the street. They arrived only seconds after it pulled into the driveway of the Golubs' house. Robert and his sister hurried inside just ahead of the mob.

The increasingly angry gathering milled outside and

continued growing in number. They shouted "murderers," then "beast." Others called out "devil raisers" and "devil people." Eight marked police cars arrived and officers formed a line between the angry crowd and the Golubs' house to maintain the peace.

Shortly after noon, Elizabeth, her daughter, and her two sons rushed from the front door to the car carrying suitcases as the crowd cheered, hooted, and jeered. As the car sped off the onlookers burst into loud applause.

About ten minutes later, John Golub, empty-handed, stone-faced, left his house as members of the crowd screamed at him. He climbed into the second car and stoically drove away to the taunts of his angry neighbors.

"What nerve," one said. "No one can believe that they came back. They came back acting as if nothing ever happened. Why would they even come back here? How can they even sleep in that house? They're not wanted here." Another suggested they should "burn the house down."

Wells had never witnessed anything like this before in a murder case and he blamed the media in large part. It had shown not the slightest consideration for the consequences of such saturation coverage of the murder and investigation. Reporters had behaved recklessly and without regard for the people who still lived on Horton Road just to sell newspapers or to get a bump in television ratings.

There was another aspect of the incident that troubled Wells. He could not believe that the conduct of neighbors and family members was serving Kelly's memory.

Is this how her parents and friends wanted to behave in her name?

And what about the other victims in the case? The children in the neighborhood were being traumatized by the details of the murder, the conduct of their parents and the increasing media frenzy. He received regular reports of children suffering from nightmares and crying for no apparent reason. A twelve-year-old friend of Kelly lived next door to the Golubs' house. Wells had observed that her bedroom window faced the house. What was it like for her sleeping at night? Couldn't anyone see how destructive this was?

Yes, an innocent girl had been savagely murdered, but there were other innocents still living here, and he was shocked that no one on Horton Road was demonstrating the slightest concern for them.

A calm settled over Horton Road for a time that evening, contrasting sharply with the frenzy of the day. But after dark, officers standing watch heard what sounded like a loud explosion coming from the Golubs' house. They ran to the side of the structure and discovered that someone had set off a huge firework inside the house. The search of the immediate area turned up no one. Additional officers were summoned and at last the neighborhood settled in for the night.

By Monday, there were those on Horton Road who expressed remorse for what had taken place over the weekend. "It is a shame what happened," one told a reporter. "It is their house. [But] I think the parents went too far when they brought the boys back." Another said, "It doesn't seem that the people who live here feel anything for the parents. When Mr. Golub came out and people started screaming at him, I started crying and I had to walk away. You bring up a child, but after a few years, that child has a mind of its own."

John Golub told reporters, "I thought we had some friends here, but I guess we don't. . . . We will have to move from here, but I'm not going to move until this is settled." He referred to the mob as "animals." Then added, "These people are not the judge and jury."

Kelly's mother, Victoria, who until now had remained publicly silent, was having no second thoughts about what had taken place and seemed to have found a target toward which to direct her grief. She now spoke up, her viewpoint representing by far the largest block in the neighborhood.

"I thought my daughter is gone and they are still walking around. These bold people. How could they just walk back like nothing happened?" she said as she sobbed. "We were all outraged."

Ten

On Tuesday, the day before the grand jury was to convene, Cotter and Wells quietly met with Richard Tinyes and his attorney to advise them of the status of the investigation. "We're going after the older brother," Cotter informed Kelly's father. "We are satisfied that the older brother did it."

Cotter went on to explain why no one else would be indicted. Acknowledging that John Jay very likely had let Kelly into the Golub house, he said this does not make him a murderer. None of the forensic evidence placed him in the basement. In addition, "The two other kids in the house provide John with an alibi. At this time, we don't believe he knows anything about the murder."

Further, there was absolutely no evidence to tie either of the two visitors or any other member of the Golub family to the killing. The matter would be taken to the grand jury the next day and until then Cotter asked that what he was telling the pair be withheld from the public.

Kelly's father was not happy with this conclusion. He wanted to know why Cotter was not calling the six-year-old neighbor girl who said she had witnessed the murder and seen others in the basement including John

Jay. The girl's father was a friend of the Tinyes family
and said he believed what his daughter told him.

Cotter responded, "There are no other witnesses than
the ones we're calling." He could only repeat that he
must act on the evidence, not on conjecture. He told
them, "We'll arrest Robert Golub as soon as the grand
jury returns an indictment."

When the grand jury filed into the courthouse in
Mineola on Wednesday, March 22, the case it was taking up was the worst-kept official secret in Valley
Stream history. That very day *Newsday* reported the
confidential meeting of the grand jury was being held
to consider the murder of Kelly Ann Tinyes and reporters spotted grand jurors entering the courthouse with
copies of *Newsday* under their arms. There was speculation as to whether one or both of the brothers would
be charged.

The *Daily News* was more direct. "WE KNOW WHO
KILLED KELLY," the headline screamed. Columnist
Mike McAlary wrote a detailed article outlining the private meeting the previous day between the prosecutor,
Wells, Richard Tinyes, and Tinyes's attorney. From the
large number of quotes and detail, it was obvious someone in the room had been wearing a tape recorder and
had given the recording to McAlary. Because of the frequency and accuracy of leaks, detectives on the case
looked at Wells with suspicion.

Nolan knew that was out of the question. Wells was
the last person in this investigation who was about to
leak anything to a media that had made his job virtually
impossible these past two weeks. The incident created

even more unrest in the investigation and it continued to be dogged by internal suspicion over who was leaking information to the press.

Indeed, a "dark cloud" hung over the investigation and the Homicide Squad in general. That was how Wells put it to Nolan. His failure to have made a speedy arrest in what, on the surface, appeared to be a simple case was creating ill will among some of the detectives. Each day when Wells arrived at his desk, someone would ask if he had made an arrest yet. Wells was sick of putting up with it and wasn't shy about letting his feelings known.

This was not the usual grand jury presentation. Customarily, a lone police officer was called to testify and the case for indictment was presented on his testimony alone. This time Cotter presented a series of witnesses to testify to the evidence. His case was comprised entirely of forensic evidence and Cotter was not prepared to risk a nonindictment because the grand jury had difficulty following what he considered to be the inescapable conclusion of that physical evidence.

So grand jurors heard from Wells, but they also heard from Steinbeck, Birdsall, and others who had gathered bits and pieces of the evidence that pointed to Robert Golub. They heard testimony from the medical examiner, from the Juvenile Aid Bureau, and from the Latent Print Section. Even members of the Tinyes family were called. In some regards it was a dry run of the trial to follow.

By 5:30 that afternoon the grand jury had heard all that Cotter had to offer and convened briefly to indict

Robert Golub for the murder of Kelly Ann Tinyes. There was no death penalty in the State of New York at the time and the maximum offense for which Robert could be indicted was second degree murder. Cotter took the indictment to the court and a warrant was issued for Robert's arrest.

The prosecutor handed the indictment and warrant to Wells in a closed envelope, and then, as if Wells were an amateur, told him this was a sealed indictment and he was to give the papers to Nolan. Wells nodded his head, but Cotter wanted to make his point even more forcefully. Cotter wanted no leaks and he swore to God if Wells opened that envelope he would see him in jail for it.

Nolan took the envelope into a meeting with the brass and for three hours a debate raged as to how to proceed while Wells stalked the hallway waiting for the go-ahead. His nerves were stretched to their absolute limit. He could not understand the delay. When Nolan came out he informed Wells his superiors had split on how to proceed. Half wanted Robert Golub arrested; the other half said to let him turn himself in.

"Then I'll break the fucking tie," Wells said as he went to issue orders for Robert to be arrested.

As word of the single indictment against the older brother leaked and then spread into the community, not everyone was satisfied they had their man. The Tinyeses were not alone in thinking that just half of the killers had been named and there was at least as much dissatisfaction as comfort in hearing the news.

Since the day he had first looked at Kelly's body,

Wells had ordered Robert placed under police surveillance. When Wells learned that Cotter would be asking for an indictment against Robert, he had instructed that the loose surveillance be tightened. He wanted his men ready to pick the suspect up the moment Wells learned the warrant had been issued for his arrest.

Robert spent the day of the grand jury in Manhattan with his older sister, Adele, and by this time was well aware that he was under close police scrutiny. As the grand jury was listening to evidence, Robert entered a large department store in downtown Manhattan. The officers following lost him when he hurried out one of several exits.

Word spread in Valley Stream that Robert Golub had been indicted, but was not in custody. Wells had his men searching everywhere for Robert but they had no luck. This was just what he had feared might happen. In his estimation Robert was capable of anything. All the dithering by the top brass had just given the young man that much time to slip their grasp.

Robert Player telephoned Wells and complained about the police department's failing to arrest Robert that day. He said the entire Tinyes family was enraged.

Nolan was called on the carpet by his superiors, some of whom had attended the earlier meeting, and was forced to defend the conduct of the men tailing Robert. He told them he was confident they would have Robert in custody momentarily. But the hours stretched until late into the night and still Robert Golub was free.

Nolan received word from Robert's attorney, John O'Grady, that his client was prepared to surrender to police the next day, a Thursday. When Wells was informed, he only increased efforts to locate the young man. He and his detectives hadn't worked all these long, exhausting hours to be denied the pleasure of slapping handcuffs on Robert. But by morning his detectives had still been unable to locate him.

That same Wednesday night John and Elizabeth Golub had been alone, sorting through a stack of Easter cards they had received. Many were from strangers who apologized for the crowd's behavior that previous Sunday.

That night was also one of intense anxiety and fear on Horton Road. Windows were shuttered, doors locked, and newly installed floodlights lit the yards until dawn.

Wells placed officers near O'Grady's office which was just down the street from the Fifth Precinct. He situated officers on every parameter street and at every entrance he could think of at the precinct itself so that Robert would be arrested if he attempted to walk up the street to surrender, or would be picked up the moment he stepped out of his car if he elected to drive. Wells was not about to let an accused murderer surrender to custody like some bad-check artist.

Police officers were not the only ones interested in Robert's surrender. So many reporters and satellite trucks were gathered around the usual entrance at the precinct near the parking lot that Wells commented it looked as if someone were filming a movie. He had never seen so many reporters in one place before.

In the twenty days since discovering the body of Kelly in the Golubs' basement, Wells had worked 158 hours of overtime. He never slept more than four hours a night and had not slept at all on many nights. His trips home consisted of a shower, nap, and change of clothes. Nolan lived so far away from Mineola that often

Kelly Ann Tinyes.
(*Courtesy of Newsday © 1989*)

Richard and Victoria Tinyes.
(*Courtesy of Audrey C. Tiernan/Newsday © 1989*)

Robert Golub, 21.
(Courtesy of Jim Peppler/Newsday © 1990)

John Jay Golub, 14, with parents John and Elizabeth, *center,*
and their attorney John J. O'Grady, *left,* leaving
Nassau County Police Headquarters.
(Courtesy of Michael Ach/Newsday © 1989)

The Golub home in Valley Stream, New York.

Police vehicle outside the Golub home.
(*Courtesy of Audrey C. Tiernan/Newsday © 1989*)

Robert Golub's bedroom.

Right: The basement of the Golub home.
Items seemed to have been simply thrown down the
stairs into the cluttered basement at the Golub home.

The bayonet-type item found at the murder scene.

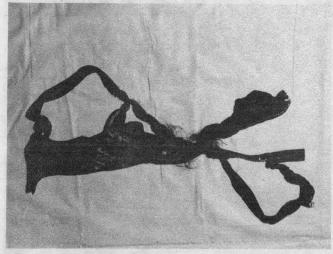

Kelly's bloodstained bra found at the scene.

Collection of black briefcases containing bloodstained clothes found in the Golub home.

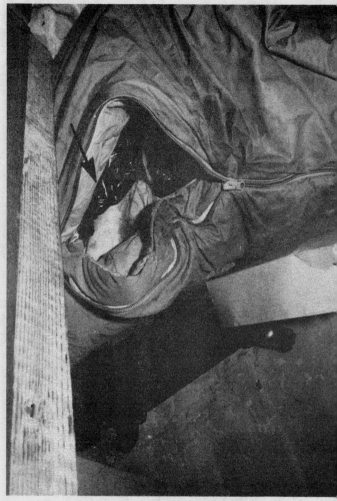
The green sleeping bag found in the Golub basement containing the mutilated body of Kelly Ann Tinyes. Arrow indicates bloodstained leg.

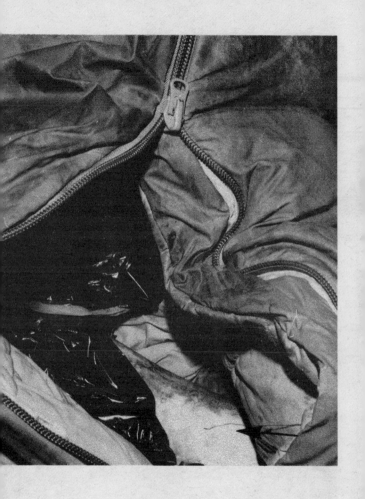

Judge Marvin Goodman.
(*Courtesy of Dick Howard/Newsday © 1989*)

The Tinyes family at the head of the procession to
Kelly's final resting place.

John and Elizabeth Golub watch as their son
Robert, *right,* is led into his bail hearing.
(*Courtesy of Dick Yarwood/Newsday © 1989*)

Nassau County Prosecutor Dan Cotter holding Kelly's picture during the closing arguments.
(*Courtesy of Dick Yarwood/Newsday* © 1990)

Victoria Tinyes and John Golub argue outside court before a hearing on harassment charges brought nearly five years after Kelly's death.
(*Courtesy of Dick Yarwood/Newsday* © 1993)

he slept on his desk or a conference table rather than drive the two-hour round-trip to shower and change. In Wells's opinion they all had the pleasure of the arrest coming to them.

But O'Grady had thought this through. His client was hurried to the main street into a car before police could make the arrest. They drove the short distance to the Fifth Precinct then stopped in a no-parking zone in front of the rarely used, largely ceremonial entrance to the building and hustled his client in for the surrender. Even the news crews who had staked out the usual parking-lot entrance were caught unprepared and had to sprint around the building to catch a shot of the suspect ducking into the building. "Here he is! Here he is!" reporters screamed as they sprinted with heavy cameras.

All the while Robert Golub repeated over and over to his lawyer, "I didn't do it, John. I didn't do it."

There was immediate and manifest relief in the neighborhood. Neighbors expressed their opinion that they had always suspected Robert. "I figured it might be him," one said. "I never thought an intruder would go into their house." Another commented, "I'm glad that someone has been implicated. Now perhaps we can get our neighborhood back . . . I felt all along that it had to be the older kid. The younger one did not have the strength to do what was done to that girl. I feel very sorry for the parents."

But Robert's friends from his high-school days expressed disbelief. "I know him," one said, "and he's not capable of doing that. I'm shocked." Another added, "I know him and I know he could not do that."

Not long after the surrender Wells escorted the prisoner out of the detention center for a hearing that day, and as he emerged into the public area he had never witnessed anything like the scene before him. He estimated two to three hundred reporters and other persons were waiting, with cameras and tape recorders. When they spotted the pair a roar rose up as reporters shouted questions, suddenly lights flashed, and spectators shouted at the pair amidst general bedlam.

As Wells pushed their way to the courtroom, a crush of reporters screamed repeatedly to a dazed Robert, who walked awkwardly with his head hung low, hands cuffed behind him. "Stand up straight! Look at the camera! Did you do it? Did you do it?"

The hearing took place in a circus atmosphere of cameras and a frenzied crowd of onlookers. Following his entry of a "not guilty" plea, Robert was ordered held in custody to await trial. He spent his first day in jail working out with weights with other prisoners. After that he was placed in isolation for his own protection.

Speaking for the Tinyes family, Robert Player stated publicly that they believed others were involved in the murder. "It's been an ordeal," Player said, adding, "Now it's basically a waiting game."

That night a group of detectives gathered at a local pub. As was the custom when an indictment was obtained in a major case, the lead detective bought everyone drinks. Wells, who no longer drank, tossed $300 on the bar, and for one night, at least, took some satisfaction in how the case was proceeding.

Now *Newsday* published the most shocking revelation to date. They had learned that Robert Golub once took a mail-order taxidermy course which had instructed him in part on how to dress out and gut a deer. The mysterious incisions on Kelly's body now appeared to have a purpose. For days rumors had circulated on Horton Road that Kelly had been gutted like an animal and her internal organs removed from her body. While this news account laid those rumors to rest, it suggested an even more gruesome possibility. Her killer had attempted to skin her like a sporting trophy.

Wells viewed this as highly speculative. He had learned that Robert had been deer hunting and had once observed the dressing out of a deer. The long cut down the length of Kelly's body and the incisions seemed to him consistent with someone trying to dress out a human body in the same fashion hunters did a deer. He believed Robert had attempted the procedure, thinking to cut Kelly into smaller parts which he could carry off undetected.

Wells believed that Robert, already exhausted from the incredible energy the killing required, had been physically unable to finish the job that he had started. Once the frenzy of the attack had lapsed and he was faced with the grim task of disembowelment and dismemberment, he had become repulsed and unable to proceed. At that point he had hidden Kelly in the sleeping bag and tried to clean up after himself.

This pointed to another aspect of this case that Wells had concluded. For nearly two weeks the technicians had gathered evidence in the Golubs' basement, their job made all the more difficult because of its chaotic condition. But in the end Wells decided that the clutter had worked to his advantage. If the basement had been clean it would have been easier for Robert to spot the blood and to have removed it more effectively. As it was, much of the blood was difficult to see and had been left behind for the police to find.

It also suggested that the conduct of the Tinyes family the Friday night they had searched so frantically for their daughter very likely made Robert's arrest more likely. He had gambled that in the dead of night he could remove Kelly from his house, but the Tinyeses and Players had canvassed the street repeatedly and there had been no opportunity to dispose of the girl. By daylight whatever chance had existed was gone.

More than once Wells had considered what would have happened if Robert had successfully removed Kelly's body from his house and dumped it miles away or in another jurisdiction. He doubted very seriously he would ever have gathered enough evidence to justify a search of the Golubs' home, let alone bring about the arrest of Robert Golub.

For weeks now Wells had come to live with the persistent taste of bile. So intense was the pressure on him that its metallic bite crept from under his tongue almost continuously. He popped antacid pills as if he were eating candy and several times he experienced a tightness about his chest, accompanied by an unpleasant, frightening sensation along the length of his left arm. For several years Wells had taken pills for high blood pressure and he understood what the symptoms were telling him. *None of that,* he said to himself, *I've got no time for that.*

Robert was arraigned on charges of murder the following week at which time O'Grady, who had been retained privately by the Golubs, withdrew as his attorney, though he would continue to represent the family's interests. He had urged the Golubs to spend their resources on an investigator and to retain experts to testify at the coming trial. Judge Marvin Goodman, who had been assigned the case for trial, appointed John Lewis, a veteran defense attorney, to serve as counsel.

Now that Robert was in custody, Cotter moved to require that he give teeth impressions before he suffered a "mouth injury." The impressions would be provided to Dr. Lowell Levine for comparison and examination with the photographs of the marks found on Kelly's body. Following a hearing at which Lewis objected to the taking of the impressions, the court issued the order.

In discussing the strength of his circumstantial case against Robert Golub, Cotter told reporters that investigators had, as yet, been unable to establish a motive in the killing. In private, Cotter had reminded Wells repeatedly during the investigation that the detective should not attempt to apply a rational explanation to an irrational act. They might never truly understand what had driven Robert the day of the killing.

To reporters Cotter went on to say Kelly had been murdered in a "frenzy" and he detailed the extent of injuries the young girl had suffered. He told them that blood other than the victim's had been discovered at the murder scene, indicating the attacker was wounded during the assault.

Lacking a confession and an eyewitness it was apparent that Cotter would have to convict Robert on a case built with circumstantial evidence, evidence that not only inexorably tied Robert to the murder, but excluded anyone else. It would be like a house of cards, each circumstantial link supporting the next so that if any fell the case itself could collapse. For this approach to succeed it was essential that the jury have absolute faith in the integrity of the investigation and in the development of the forensic evidence.

Key to the prosecution would be the use of DNA tests of the various blood samples taken from the Golub family, from Kelly, and from the basement. Cotter could not be certain if sufficient quantities of blood existed in the samples taken from the crime scene for Lifecodes to perform its analysis.

DNA, or deoxyribonucleic acid, is the basic genetic code found in all cells. With the exception of identical twins, no two individuals' DNA is the same. The quantity of tissue required for testing had been decreasing at a rapid rate since the process was first developed. In 1989 the sample was the size of a dime.

In DNA testing a blood sample is dissected by enzymes which are then spread on an electrified gel. Polymorphism patterns resembling an abacus are produced on an X-ray photograph and can pinpoint from whom the blood came as well as identify from whom the blood could not have come.

Lifecodes, the firm which would be performing the DNA tests for the prosecution, had been founded in 1982 and became the first American laboratory to offer commercial forensic DNA testing in late 1986. By 1989, DNA matches had been used in about two thousand criminal cases and Lifecodes had provided the results in fifteen hundred of those cases. Though DNA testing was accepted in twenty-seven states it remained controversial, not because the underlying theory was questioned by the scientific community, but because some aspects of the procedure still depended on human handling. While prosecutors liked to label the results "DNA fingerprinting," defense attorneys criticized its susceptibility to improper processing, subjective analysis, and general mishandling.

A second key piece of circumstantial evidence in this case was the palmprint lifted from the closet molding which the FBI had confirmed as Robert's. Palmprints, however, were notorious in law enforcement for their unreliability because unlike fingerprints, which are a unique pattern of ridges, palmprints are assessed based on folds of the skin which do not have the same highly individual character.

Cotter was going to have to convince a jury this particular palmprint, small as it was, had come from Robert. And if it was his, that it had been made in blood at the time of the murder. There was no way, in fact, to establish just how long the print had been in existence.

Last were the apparent bite marks found on Kelly's body. Results of a comprehensive analysis could not be available until shortly before the trial since the examination was a painstaking, highly subjective procedure that depended in large part on the expertise of the examiner.

Lowell Levine, the Huntington odontologist conducting the examination, had made his reputation by matching the teeth that led to the identification of Nazi war criminal Joseph Mengele, and had determined that teeth marks on victims in Florida had come from the notorious serial killer Ted Bundy.

Robert Golub might be in jail, but there was a great deal to accomplish if he was going to stay there.

Twenty-three days following the murder of their daughter, Richard and Victoria Tinyes granted reporters an in-depth interview. So much had been taking place, Richard acknowledged, "We really haven't had time to mourn Kelly."

The couple said they were not convinced that Robert Golub had acted alone. "We feel a little relieved that he was arrested," Victoria said. "But the investigation is continuing, and we're not completely satisfied."

"Our lives have been turned upside down," Richard said. "There isn't a moment we don't think about her or what happened."

The parents had asked themselves repeatedly what the caller had said to Kelly to persuade her to go to the Golubs' house, and they thought endlessly about what had happened to their daughter once she went inside.

"I've asked God, Why? And why Kelly?" Victoria said. "I just have to think that she's at peace now."

Eleven

On March 31 John and Elizabeth quietly moved back into their house on Horton Road, this time without their sons and without incident. In the days to follow they were generally shunned by neighbors and stuck to themselves as they attempted to go about their everyday lives.

Because Horton Road was a one-way street, it was impossible for the two families to avoid one another. Each day both Richard and Victoria Tinyes were forced to drive in front of the Golubs' residence, and Richard passed John's service station en route to his own business which was in the same area. When the Golubs returned home from work, they passed the Tinyeses' house and it was not uncommon for Victoria to stand in her yard and glare at them as they drove slowly down Horton Road on their regular routine.

It was apparent that the Tinyes family found no relief in the arrest of Robert Golub. Increasingly, they vented their anger against the mother and father of the accused killer. Elizabeth and John infuriated them by their steadfast refusal to abandon their home, and their stated belief in their son's innocence.

In early April, John Jay, whom police still identified as a suspect, quietly moved back into his parents' house.

The next night the window to his bathroom was shattered by what proved to be a pellet fired from the street. Shortly after that the Golubs sent their youngest son away to boarding school.

At this time Wells experienced a sharp pain in his chest much worse than the others, a pain so intense he nearly doubled over. His face broke into a cold sweat and he was left gasping when it passed. This time Pierce was with him. "You ought to get that checked out," he said, a look of concern on his face. Wells said he would—when he had the time.

On April 7 Wells and another detective went to the jail with a court order, handcuffed Robert Golub, and escorted him to a dental lab at Meadowbrook Hospital where the impressions of his teeth were to be taken. There were strict departmental rules against posing a prisoner for photographs or allowing the prisoner to pose himself so the men just moved through the crowd of reporters who met them as they walked to the car then followed them in a parade to the hospital. They arrived before Robert's attorney so the detectives waited with Robert already in the chair and Levine with his assistant standing by.

Robert looked at Wells. "How do you sleep at nights?" he asked.

"I sleep good. How do you sleep at nights?"

"You know you got the wrong man here."

"I do? Then tell me who the right guy is. I'll be

more than happy to go out and catch him, but right now you look like you are the only game in town here."

"Well, it could have been someone else."

"What do you want me to think, Robert?" Wells replied. "That a masked murderer dressed as a Ninja flew in his Lear jet and landed in a field near your house, snuck in, called Kelly, and murdered her in your basement with no one's knowledge?"

Robert was silent for a moment. Then, "I didn't do it."

This time Wells said nothing. Shortly afterward the lawyer arrived and Levine went to work. He installed a metal device to spread Robert's lips then took photographs of his teeth. After this Levine had him bite into a wax preparation. Finally, the odontologist took molds of Robert's upper and lower teeth. The procedures took over an hour before Wells escorted his prisoner back to jail.

In some ways it seemed the Golubs' house itself would be on trial, though not in the way many on Horton Road seemed to think. It would be necessary to demonstrate to a jury how Kelly could be so brutally murdered in the basement while others in the house heard nothing. The evidence said Kelly had been slaughtered in a room in the basement. On top of that rock music had been blasting throughout the house.

To aid in the prosecution it would be helpful for the jury to visualize where each key piece of evidence had been discovered and to satisfy themselves that five people could have moved in different directions in the house without detecting one another.

Some months earlier, in a sensational murder trial, a retired police officer and former crime-scene cartographer named Charles Fox had constructed a re-creation of the block where the killing of a police officer had taken place. Nolan knew the detective who had worked the case from his bagpipe band and spoke to him about the effectiveness of the reconstruction during the trial. Nolan informed Wells and Cotter. Cotter thought it an excellent idea and spoke to Fox to see if he would do the same thing in this case.

What the prosecutor initially had in mind was a large-scale reconstruction of the Golubs' house and of Horton Road. He would use it to assist the jury in visualizing the movements of the five persons who were key to understanding what had taken place the Friday of the murder. Fox quoted a figure that caused Cotter to blanch so he settled for a one-twelfth-scale model of the Golubs' house, designed in such a way that portions could be removed to allow a scrutiny of the interior. Fox went to work at once, spending weeks measuring and examining the Golubs' house and constructing his scale model.

The days following Robert's indictment had allowed no respite for Wells. Toward the end of another exhausting day he and Pierce were in the homicide squad room in Mineola when Wells lifted a large case file. As he started to walk he experienced the now familiar chest pain again. This time it froze him in place and the file tumbled to the floor. Pierce said, "I told you to get that checked out."

A sergeant was in the room. Seeing the look on

Wells's face he said, "Why don't you call the ambulance?"

The pain was so excruciating that Wells was frozen in place, unable to move even to fall down. Finally he could speak. "Naw, I don't want to make a big deal out of this." The words required all of his effort. "I can go to the doctor later on." Pierce had sent for the ambulance anyway. Wells refused to be carried off the job and walked awkwardly down the stairs to the ambulance accompanied by the sergeant.

He lay on a stretcher and the paramedic put an EKG on him and took his blood pressure. The next thing Wells remembered was the paramedic drawing blood and taping vials to his chest. "Do you know how to drive an ambulance?" the lone paramedic asked the sergeant who answered that he did not. "Get behind the wheel anyway and drive us to the hospital as fast as you can."

At the hospital Wells was placed in the trauma room and placed on an IV. He remained there for seven hours still fully clothed while doctors monitored him constantly. Late that night he was moved into a room and the nurse told him to try and sleep. A few moments later nurses and doctors stormed into the room and began emergency resuscitation efforts in the bed next to Wells. When they failed the body was wheeled out.

Just as Wells nodded off a second time, a priest arrived at the request of his wife. He said he understood Wells was a Catholic. "When was the last time you were in church?" he asked.

"Not counting weddings, twenty-five years."

With an understanding nod of his head the priest administered the Last Rites.

* * *

Oh April 25, seven weeks after the murder of Kelly Ann Tinyes, Lewis argued once again that Robert be released on bail pending trial. Cotter opposed, telling the court that the People's case "relies heavily on known witnesses that live nearby." If Robert was released from custody those people believed that he posed a "grave risk to their safety." He told the court that the neighbors on Horton Road were "almost held hostage within their neighborhood out of fear that this act might be committed on someone else in the neighborhood."

Lewis disagreed, saying it was the Golubs who lived in fear. "The Golub family was the subject of something fired at a window, cherry bombs, garbage being dumped on the lawn, and threats made to the family," he told the court.

When the judge set bail at a prohibitive $5 million, the crowd attending the hearing broke into wild applause. Elizabeth Golub, who had dropped a considerable amount of weight by this time, was sitting to the rear of the courtroom with her husband and daughter. Hearing the decision, she began to sob. A few moments later as Elizabeth left the courtroom, Linda Player shot an angry remark at her. Elizabeth turned and yelled back, "I'm a parent too!"

In the hallway she told a reporter, "We're all parents. I'm not an animal! We want justice, too. What would any parent in my position do?"

That day Elizabeth Golub and her husband granted their first interview to reporters, describing how they were virtually prisoners in their own home. Their daughter's wedding had been postponed because of the trauma.

Nearly every day a crowd gathered outside their house and glared at them. When they drove down the street after visiting their son, they were routinely jeered at. Twice, Elizabeth claimed, she had nearly been run off the road by one of her neighbors.

The couple told the reporter that they mourned for Kelly and they felt they were being unfairly portrayed in news accounts. "We want this crime solved as much as they do. But we want a chance to investigate and prove our son is innocent. They seem to think we don't care. That's very far from the truth. We do care. What would any other parent do?"

John Golub reminded the reporter that his family had voluntarily vacated their house for two weeks so the police could scour it for clues. Every day he read in the paper new developments and was sick to his stomach as he learned of them. Recently someone had taken to tossing garbage onto their lawn.

"Now, all of a sudden [people] are condemning me, and my family. If this happened to them, I would never say a word to him other than to offer him sympathy. If it was his son that was accused, I would never blame him or his wife or his daughter. . . ."

Elizabeth defended her household, saying the news accounts made no mention of the Christian magazines they had in their home, or of the books of poetry, the china or cut glass.

"I understand the pain that Vicky is going through," she said. "I pray for them every night . . . I pray for the soul of Kelly. And I pray for my family."

Linda Player had a ready response when the reporter asked her about the incidents. "I don't know what she's talking about. She's probably imagining these things."

Player admitted that in good weather neighbors did often congregate in front of the Golubs' house, but denied anyone in the neighborhood was harassing the Golubs. She made it clear that "no one wants to see them on that block."

The reaction to the printing of the Golubs' story was immediate. A petition was presented to a newspaper and a local television station representing nine of the families which lived on the street, though they refused to name themselves.

"We will not bother the Golub family," the statement read. "We never have, but we are sincere in our belief that they don't belong on Horton Road. . . . We find it hard to believe that they could return with the air of bravado and lack of feeling and respect for the Tinyes family that they have displayed. . . ."

Most of all the petitioners were "especially disturbed that attention has been shifted away from the crime . . . in exchange for the inaccurate and unfounded charges of harassment by the Golubs."

Other neighbors, who also asked not to be identified, expressed empathy for the Golubs. They said the Golubs had the right to stand by their son and to defend the family.

Life on Horton Road had been dramatically and tragically altered by events. Religious zealots were circulating leaflets announcing the Apocalypse had arrived, and strangers drove or walked down the street daily to gaze at the Golubs' house. The children acknowledged being frightened and for the most part maintained a wide berth of the "death house," as the Golubs' home was commonly known.

Many of the parents were openly expressing anger at

the Golubs, and young children confessed it made them uncomfortable. "Some people say knock down the house and I agree with that," one ten-year-old said. "All I think of when I look at the house is how they killed her and what they did to her and, like, I can see it."

The children were also excited by the media's attention. When reporters canvassed the neighborhood searching for human interest stories, they insisted their names appear in the newspaper, unlike their parents who preferred anonymity regardless of which side they were taking. At school, the children said, they were celebrities because they lived on Horton Road, knew Kelly, and had seen Robert.

The initial reaction of the adult neighbors had been an automatic sympathy for the Tinyes family with some lesser affinity for the Golubs. Events had caused most families to ally with the Tinyeses, and there were those of the group eager to make this a witch-hunt.

But recent events had seen a retreat from the Tinyes family by several neighbors, and by summer the families were divided roughly equally in their feelings. If the truth was known, most of them likely wished both families would just move away.

Newsday ran an editorial calling on the neighbors to stop blaming the family for what one member had allegedly done. However no mention was made about the impact of the paper's emotion-charged articles and relentless street reports on the once quiet community.

For thirteen days Wells remained in the hospital recovering from a heart attack. The first time Nolan came to visit he said, "God damn it, if you die, I swear I'll kill you." Wells laughed even though it hurt.

The doctor told Wells the attack had been stress related and he was very lucky to be alive. As he lay in the hospital Wells experienced little fear of death. He was more frightened than he had ever been in his life that he might be so disabled that he could no longer be a police officer.

When Wells was released without surgery and placed on medication, Nolan put him on restrictive assignment. Wells agreed to limit his duty, then promptly went back to doing what he had done before. After a few weeks he quit carrying his nitroglycerin tablets.

Routine, procedural hearings were taking place every few weeks throughout the summer and drew packed courtrooms, roughly divided equally between supporters of the Tinyes and Golub families. Rather than ease hostilities, tension grew and police expressed fears that the murder of Kelly Ann Tinyes might only be the first on Horton Road.

In August the Nassau County District Attorney's Office received a petition signed by eighteen persons living on Horton Road, outlining what they claimed was a pattern of harassment they and their children had suffered at the hands of John and Elizabeth Golub. The petition was not signed by the Tinyes family, but by neighbors who strongly supported them.

The residents claimed that over Memorial Day weekend John Jay Golub had given three children, including the six-year-old who said she had seen him murder Kelly along with the entire Golub family, "a threatening look. He then jumped inside the door [to his house] with his parents standing behind him and continued to make these threatening faces at them." The petition claimed that the next day John Jay stood on the stoop of his house and "made faces" at Richie Tinyes and Sharon Stonel.

Two weeks later Sharon's father, a signatory on the petition, was working on his roof when he noticed a package in his front yard. According to the petitioners, it was a package which had been mailed to him. He spotted John Golub standing nearby and he admitted that he had pitched the package which was marked "fragile" onto his yard. John Golub then "gave Mr. Stonel the finger."

Three families on Horton Road alleged they had received threatening telephone calls including some saying their houses would be firebombed if the Golubs were not left alone.

The petition claimed John Golub had also "given the neighbors the finger for no apparent reason," and that his wife had made a threatening face at Sharon Stonel.

The petition then recounted in detail an incident which was alleged to have occurred on August 10 in which Elizabeth Golub had taken photographs of Richard Tinyes and a friend of the Golubs had also taken photographs of neighborhood children. After observing the street for a time, Elizabeth Golub drove down it, followed by her friends in their own car. Elizabeth held a tape recorder out the car window and as she passed the recorder played, "Monster mother! Monster mother!" over and over in a child's voice.

The petition concluded by saying, "We feel these tactics are being used to intimidate these children in order to scare them from testifying and applying pressure to their parents to possibly withdraw them from the case." The petition asked for an order of protection from the Golubs and their friends, and for additional police protection on Horton Road. No order was forthcoming, but more police were assigned to watch the neighborhood.

Every day Wells arrived at work and speculated with Pierce as to what it would be today. Would someone give the finger to someone else? Who would claim he had been threatened. You never knew. It was no longer possible for Wells to eat a meal at home without interruption. Someone from the office would call to say, "Richard Tinyes is complaining that the Golubs are back in the house and you better get over there to do something." Wells would go to see Richard Tinyes and listen to his latest complaint. Then he would attempt to smooth the situation over. It was as if Richard thought Wells was his own private police department.

In mid-August hearings were held to determine if Robert's statements to police would be admitted at trial. Detectives testified that Robert had told them that his brother, John Jay, and Kelly were "an item"—he could see it "in their eyes"—and that on three occasions in the weeks before her murder, Robert had taken telephone calls from Kelly for his brother. He also denied any knowledge of the bloody bayonet found at the murder scene.

Cotter told the court that these statements were demonstratively false. Telephone records revealed no calls to or from either the Golubs' or Tinyeses' houses during the period when Robert claimed he received them for his brother. There were many friends of both Kelly and John Jay able to testify that no intimate relationship existed between the pair, and finally, neighborhood children would testify that they had seen the bayonet in Robert's possession. "These statements will be contradicted . . . and will show a consciousness of guilt in giving false explanations to police."

John Lewis argued that his client, who had been sitting impassively throughout the hearings, had been subjected to expert questioning by police officers with more than "two hundred years of police experience," and that the officers had been careful to write down only these answers that served the objectives of the investigation. The interviews had not been recorded.

"How do we know what was actually said there? We certainly know that anything that was good for the boy was left out."

For the first time the public learned of the two marks found on Kelly's body, which the prosecution believed were caused by biting. When Cotter announced their existence during the hearing, a moan rose from the audience. Cotter informed the court that the examination of all forensic evidence would soon be completed and that the people would be ready for trial.

Lewis told the judge that Robert claimed the police had used force during his questioning. Wells took the stand and denied that any abuse had taken place, in particular to deny that he had leaned on Robert's groin during his questioning.

Robert's stoic facade crumbled this one time and he shouted at the judge that the police had done other things, but was quickly silenced by Lewis. The court ruled the statements and evidence would be admissible and set the trial for October 30. Lewis expressed his anger at the prosecution's unfair rush to get the case to trial and said he doubted that he could be ready so soon.

On August 14, in the midst of these proceedings, a shouting match ensued when the Golubs attempted to sit in two open seats in the front row which were co-incidentally near the Tinyes family. The Tinyeses objected that they had no right to be there. One of Kelly's grandfathers shouted an obscenity at Elizabeth Golub and raised his fist at the couple. Court officers rushed over to restore calm. A shoving match began as officers struggled to separate the milling groups. When they escorted the grandfather out of the courtroom, one officer was crushed against a doorjamb and had to be taken to a hospital for treatment.

Outside in the hallway an angry Richard Tinyes complained, "They [the Golubs] try to intimidate us. It's nonstop. They're harassing children in the neighborhood. They come down, start taking pictures of all the kids who are witnesses."

John Golub responded by saying that vandals had ripped up a portion of his lawn and their garbage cans had been run over on the sidewalk. Elizabeth, no longer the retiring housewife most people recalled, claimed that neighbors had blocked the street so she could not drive past. Others had made lewd gestures and one unidentified man had stood in the middle of Horton Road and exposed himself to her. The family's lawyer had told them to try and gather evidence and the Golubs now carried cameras and snapped photographs whenever they thought harassment was about to begin.

Despite the pleas of the Golub family for consideration, the incidents only continued. In mid-September a police officer observed Richard Tinyes using his tow truck to block the sidewalk at the Golubs' home. Two days later a crowd of thirty gathered on the Golubs' lawn shouting obscenities at the family. They came back the next day to repeat the incident. Two weeks later paint was splattered on the Golubs' cars and a brick was thrown through their front window. There seemed to be no end to what *Newsday* was now calling, "The Horror on Horton Road."

Twelve

On October 2, 1989, just four weeks from the scheduled start of the murder trial, John Lewis, Robert
Golub's court-appointed lawyer, informed Judge Goodman that he could not possibly be ready to go to trial.
He made a motion that the trial be moved until sometime in January 1990.

Cotter opposed any continuance, citing his concern
that a delay could very well inflame an already volatile
situation on Horton Road.

Judge Marvin Goodman was a native of Queens and
a graduate of City College. Following service in the
Second World War he had attended law school on the
GI bill. He had served as both a prosecutor and as a
defense attorney. A Republican, Goodman had first been
elected to the bench in 1973 and six years later was
elected to a ten-year term. He was generally regarded
as a fair judge.

After listening to the motion Judge Goodman denied
the defense's request. A heated exchange ensued during
which an exasperated Lewis told the judge, "I will not
be forced to trial. You might as well hold me on contempt and put me in jail."

"You asked to be relieved?" Goodman asked.

"Yes."

"You're relieved. You haven't given me any legal reasons [regarding his preparation time] . . . You had over nine weeks to get ready."

The following day Judge Goodman appointed experienced and aggressive attorney Salvatore Marinello to replace him. Marinello was a former county prosecutor and the former chief of the Queens District Attorney's Homicide Squad. To allow him time to prepare, the trial was delayed until January.

Cotter and Marinello had shared the same office at the Nassau County District Attorney's Office when the attorney worked there. The two lawyers shared a common love of fine cigars, had a similar sense of humor, and the same love of food. "We had a good time," Marinello said when asked about the ten years during which he and Cotter had shared a cramped office. "We had two desks in an office that should only have had one. . . . It was difficult but we managed to cooperate. . . . We consider ourselves good friends and also consummate professionals."

Both attorneys were known for their meticulous preparation. In murder trials friends very often made for the best adversaries. Three times previously Marinello had represented an accused killer when Cotter had been the prosecutor. In 1986 Marinello had defended a man accused of killing an Israeli folksinger, then he had defended a man charged with setting a rooming-house fire that caused the deaths of five people, and just the previous summer he had defended a man charged with the beating death of a woman. The decisions had been one-sided to date. Cotter had obtained convictions in all three cases along with the imposition of maximum sentences.

John Golub was distressed at the removal of Lewis as was Robert, who voiced his objection to the court.

Following the announcement of Marinello's appointment, John told reporters in the hallway that his son was "frightened. He thinks the system is going to frame him."

While he spoke Elizabeth Golub clutched her husband's hand and nervously eyed a group of Tinyes supporters gathering around them. As the crowd began heckling, court officers escorted the Golubs through them and out of the courthouse.

Immediately after being named to represent Robert Golub, Marinello went on the offensive. He had never previously been involved in a criminal trial so dependent on scientific evidence. What was admitted and what was excluded before the trial even began could be essential to the defense.

In a series of hearings during the fall of 1989, Marinello challenged every key aspect of the People's case. First, he questioned the legality of the search of the Golub home, charging the Golubs had signed the consent under duress.

Elizabeth Golub took the stand and testified that the Saturday Kelly's body was found in her basement "was the worst day of my life." She claimed she was too upset to know what she was doing and had no recollection of what she said to police officers when they requested permission to search her house. She denied even reading the consent form.

Under cross-examination Elizabeth had difficulty remembering events and frequently contradicted herself. Asked why she had signed the consent form authorizing the search, she tearfully testified that she had not known what she was doing. She was very distraught, so much so that at one point during her testimony Robert gestured with his hands for his mother to calm herself.

Victoria Tinyes sat in the courtroom crying during the testimony. "She's just evading everything," she said. "She's afraid of something."

Marinello also attacked the search warrant obtained later that day, asserting that no probable cause existed to justify the warrant. He also claimed most of the physical evidence had been gathered from the Golubs' house before the warrant was issued and that officers were lying to cover themselves.

Each of these hearings was attended by angry spectators and court security officers were now careful to separate the two factions, seating them on different sides of the courtroom. So intense were emotions that Elizabeth Golub passed out in the courtroom at one point during testimony. On November 3 Robert mouthed words toward his mother. Victoria Tinyes, who was in attendance, shot to her feet and shouted, "You should be in a cage with handcuffs! He doesn't have the privilege to talk to anybody! Just remember what you did!"

Robert turned to face her with a grin on his face. Victoria screamed as if he had touched her. "Don't you look at me! Don't you look at me!" After initially resisting her friends who stepped forward to calm her, she was escorted from the courtroom.

One week later the court upheld the validity of the search of the Golubs' house. The Tinyes parents breathed audible sighs of relief while a grim-faced John Golub sat on the other side of the courtroom from them. As he was being led away Linda Player shouted at Robert repeatedly, "Does it refresh your memory? Is your memory refreshed?"

Finally, Marinello attacked the admissibility of the DNA tests, resulting in a series of protracted hearings. On November 27, during such a proceeding, Robert turned his head toward Victoria Tinyes once again. This time he mouthed an obscenity at her.

The incidents outside the courtroom on Horton Road continued without respite. On November 14 a window in the Golub house was broken, followed by a message which John Golub tape-recorded. "How do you like it? How do you like the broken window?"

Two days later both the telephone and power lines to the Golub home were cut. On November 28 Victoria Tinyes was reported to have driven her car directly at John Golub. On Christmas Eve three windows in the Golub home were shattered.

These incidents were reported to the police and others as well, but either nothing had taken place that was against the law or no suspects could be identified.

Nolan's assignment of George Pierce to assist Wells had proven inspired. Pierce had prepared the flowcharts for which Wells had no patience and had been the one to announce that they could prove in court that only Robert Golub had the opportunity to kill Kelly, because the time frame was right only for him. He had seen to the thousand details that would prove so important to the prosecution.

John Golub had nagged Wells throughout the summer about his collection of antique pocket watches. None had been discovered in his bedroom where he said he

kept some and there had been none in the attaché cases.
As he persisted and the tempers on Horton Road heightened, Wells expressed his frustration with the constant
questions about the watches. He could just see his men
being accused of stealing thousands of dollars' worth of
watches.

Pierce took it on himself to solve the mystery. He
canvassed the pawn shops in the vicinity and discovered
the watches. Robert Golub had pawned his father's collection the day before the murder.

The scale model of the Golubs' house had at last
been delivered. Cotter was delighted with the end prod-
uct and had the structure placed in his office. The model
house was three feet wide by four feet deep by two and
a half feet high. It easily disassembled into convenient
parts. The walls were of brick and stone, the roof finished in asphalt shingles. It was so large most of Cotter's furniture had to be shoved against the walls, but
he paid no attention to the inconvenience.

Nearly everyone the prosecutor saw at work was required to come into his office and praise his pride and
joy. Cotter demonstrated how the model was taken apart
and how he could track the course of events the day of
the killing in this way. Others had blanched when informed of the cost, but Cotter considered the model worth
every dollar of the $4,500 it had cost the taxpayers.

As the trial date approached, attention focused increasingly on courtroom security. Six wooden barriers
were borrowed from the police and two and a half times

the usual number of court security officers were assigned, not to provide security for Robert Golub or the judge, but to separate the feuding families.

"With the tensions between the two families, we think violence is a real possibility," the chief clerk said. "We have to do everything we can to try and keep them apart."

The court had done a largely ineffective job of preventing outbursts between the families up to this point. The difficulty lay in the fact that both sets of parents were morally allowed to witness the proceedings, and Judge Goodman would only prevent their presence as a last resort.

There was a heightened sense of the need for security as well because the trial, with its graphic details, would be broadcast over television. Hoping to curb the sensationalism as much as possible, the court ruled that there would be no audio broadcast of the medical examiner's testimony or of any testimony regarding alleged teeth marks. For the jurors' protection their names were not released and cameras were not permitted to film them.

During the weeks approaching the trial both Wells and Pierce had been busy men. Cotter wanted as much of the case as possible reduced to charts and graphs. The men also brought the young witnesses who would be testifying to the courtroom during nonworking hours to explain to them where everyone would be sitting, how the trial was conducted, and to familiarize themselves with the scene. This was intended to make them as comfortable as possible when they testified.

Given the unprecedented publicity and the public pressure, Wells continued working a great deal of overtime. This was becoming a source of irritation with the other homicide detectives who had their own important cases but were restricted in the hours they could put in. Wells suspected all the attention he was receiving accounted for some of the reaction as well.

Every time his photograph appeared in the newspaper, his wife's coworkers cut it out and pinned the picture on the bulletin board at the hospital where she worked. Nolan too was so recognized from his frequent television statements and photographs in the newspaper that he was routinely stopped on the street by strangers wanting confirmation he was "that guy."

Wells was increasingly anxious as the trial date approached. He had always been uncomfortable with a case built entirely on circumstantial evidence. There was no doubt of Robert's guilt in his mind, but he knew that Cotter faced a formidable task in presenting the detailed evidence to lay jurors in such a manner that they could understand it and its implications.

An entire room at the District Attorney's Office was reserved just for the physical evidence in this case, and it was here that most of the pretrial preparation occurred. It was not unusual for Cotter to be interviewing a prospective witness in one corner, while Pierce had a second in his corner, and Wells was talking to still a third in his place.

To be certain Wells was available to assist him every day to prepare for the trial, Cotter issued him a subpoena. When Nolan's superiors wanted to know why Wells wasn't working other cases, he explained they had no choice, the assistant district attorney had subpoenaed Wells.

Marinello had his concerns as well. Nassau County

was in his words "a tremendously conservative community," and the Kelly Ann Tinyes murder had received saturation media coverage from the first day. Any person accused of her murder was going to face a very tough jury.

Typically citizens avoided serving on juries and answered questions during the selection process that would tend to excuse them. Marinello had found that to be especially true in the case of a high-profile trial. But those persons who wanted to be on the jury in such cases tended not to be forthcoming when questioned and proved to be those with "preconceived notions."

His late assignment to the case bothered him as well. It was not unusual for a murder trial in Nassau County to be held a year, even two years following an arrest. Judge Goodman had them going to trial in less than ten months. The media attention had created a sense of urgency that would not have existed in other cases.

As the selection of jurors began on February 5, 1990, there were genuine concerns whether a jury would be able to convict Robert. Dressed in a conservative blue suit with a calm, pleasing demeanor, he seemed the antithesis of a depraved criminal. For all the confidence Cotter expressed publicly, he faced a formidable task in persuading the jury first that key blood samples were Robert Golub's and Kelly Tinyes's, and second that they could be matched in such a sequence as to support his theory of the murder.

Marinello had gathered his own expert witnesses and they could be expected to counter, or at the least cloud, the testimony the state was prepared to bring. Cotter had one shot to lead a jury through the forensic evidence and the sophisticated world of DNA analysis, and he was apprehensive at the prospect.

The reality of juries that played to Cotter's advantage and the problem he faced were best articulated by an experienced defense attorney on the eve of the trial. "The jury will be inclined to convict in [the Golub] case because the manner in which she was killed is so gruesome. The problem with the prosecution's case is that it rests with the experts. If they don't hold up under cross-examination the case will fall apart."

The eleven months since the murder of Kelly Ann Tinyes had altered the lives of the Tinyes and Golub families beyond all recognition. In both homes the mothers held the bedroom of their missing child unchanged, almost as a shrine.

As the trial loomed Victoria Tinyes often told her surviving son that Kelly was in a better place. To others she added, "But if they say there is a hell, we are living in that hell right now."

Just five houses up the street Elizabeth Golub felt very much the same. "I've been called every name in the book," she said. "You want to know something? Those little children who call me names, I'm afraid of them."

Police had responded to countless calls for assistance since Kelly had been carried from the Golubs' basement. Fifteen written complaints had been filed with police. A local police inspector expressed his apprehension and spoke for all the police who worked Horton

Road when he said, "It is a very charged environment down there."

The lives of the neighbors had been altered as well and every family on Horton Road was a virtual prisoner since no one would buy a house on the street knowing what was taking place. Each family still had their supporters, but most of the families undoubtedly just wanted a return to normalcy.

The character of the once quiet street was altered as well. Parents were reluctant to allow their children to play outside their houses, or with the children of Horton Road. "I prefer my daughter doesn't play with the children on the block anymore," one mother explained, "because now they play games of murder and guns and shootings and stabbings."

Parents told of the nightmares from which their youngsters suffered and how children refused to sleep alone while others slept fully clothed. There were times when the fear among the children was palpable.

The pending trial brought no solace to the Tinyes and Golub fathers, either. "We still have so many questions," Richard Tinyes said. "No one deserves to die the way she did. No one deserves such a horrible death." Suspicions that John Jay was involved in the murder were stronger now than ever.

John Golub related the harassment he and his wife had suffered. "They claim they're frightened of us, but if you're frightened of me, would you go out of your way to harass me every day? . . . If I could afford it . . . I would sell to the type of people they accuse us of being. I would put someone in the house who was an animal and see how they would like it."

With all the rancor and bitterness it was too easy to

overlook how similar this horrible experience was for both families. Elizabeth Golub came closest when she said, "I'm a mother too. I feel for [Victoria]. I understand that there is a child dead who she'll never replace. I know she will hurt in that courtroom. What she doesn't understand is I'm going to hurt too."

Thirteen

In anticipation that many prospective jurors would be unable to serve on the jury of a lengthy trial or would be disqualified from serving because of the saturation media coverage of the investigation, the clerk of the court summoned an unusually large pool. So many, in fact, that the court's answering machine broke under the strain caused by handling the incoming calls.

A pool of 461 persons initially appeared in court and after the first day's screening during which Judge Goodman cautioned that the trial was expected to last for six weeks, just eighty-two remained. Sixteen more were selected the next day, and sixteen additional prospective jurors were chosen from another pool of 125. From those remaining the final selection took place.

At this point inconvenience and a predisposition toward the case had excluded most of the possible jurors, but more than one elected not to participate for personal reasons. "I decided I would rather not get that close to this case," one said. "There are enough horrors around. You read about it every day in the papers. Why put yourself through it?"

In questioning one prospective juror Cotter had acknowledged that he had difficulty sleeping some nights when his thoughts dwelled on the evidence in the case.

The selection took eight days before a jury of nine men and three women with four alternates was seated.

Throughout the process Marinello had repeatedly argued that even with a pool of six hundred persons it was not possible for an impartial jury to be selected in this case, not in Nassau County. He moved once again for a change of venue and Judge Goodman once more denied his request. As the jury was seated Marinello filed a special action in the Appellate Division of the State Supreme Court, but it was rejected as well.

The names of the jury were withheld from the public, but in the coming weeks reporters were able to obtain specifics about each member from the judge. The foreman was a twenty-one year-old bank teller. Also on the jury was a school administrator who was married and had three children, a floor supervisor, and a homemaker who often watched the Home Shopping Club on television. Altogether five of the twelve jurors were in their twenties, one was thirty-one, three were in their forties, two in their fifties, and the oldest was seventy-five.

Opening arguments began on Thursday, February 15, 1990. The trial was carried live by a local all-news television station, News 12 Long Island, and intermittently by other stations. Only one television camera would be permitted and two still photographers. No pictures could be taken of the jurors, nor could they be publicly identified.

Of special concern was the impact on the students of the Hewlett-Woodmere Schools whose superintendent had asked the court for such restrictions because of the trauma graphic depictions could cause those who had known Kelly. One student said, "I think it would totally destroy a person who was close to someone. God forbid, if that happened to my best friend, I don't think I could handle it."

Indeed, Kelly's best friend, Roberta Grosse, was having trouble dealing with the trial. She had asked herself a thousand times, "Why do such bad things happen to such wonderful people?" She could not think of Kelly without crying. "I'm angry," she told a friend. "I always will be. She was supposed to have a great sweet sixteen, and go to the prom, graduate from high school, go on to college, eventually get married, have children. All these things were just wiped away and why? That's the thing I can never understand." With the media attention of the investigation and now television coverage of the actual trial, it became increasingly difficult for her to cope with the emotions inside her.

Roberta had been outraged when she learned the Golubs planned to remain where they were. "Wouldn't they want peace of mind? Wouldn't they want to move out? Why would they want to live in an area where [emotions] are so heated? You are talking about a house where someone was murdered and they're living now in a community of hate, everyone around them hates them. . . . Why would you ever want to live where you are hated?"

Roberta vowed not to follow any portion of the trial, and her friends knew better than to say anything to her about it, but she could not help hearing explicit details of Kelly's last moments and she found them profoundly disturbing.

The image Robert Golub projected as he sat facing his jury was carefully cultivated. He wore a three-piece navy blue suit with muted pinstripes and a crisp white shirt with a conservative tie. His dark brown hair was meticulously combed and just touched the collar of his shirt. His dark eyes and lush eyelashes were nearly feminine in aspect and he held himself very still, as if he were unconcerned by the proceeding, any nervousness displayed only by his incessantly blinking eyes.

In Nassau County lawyers address the court from lecterns so Cotter stood at his place to deliver the People's opening argument to the jury. Not far from where he stood was a cardboard box containing several attaché cases.

Cotter described the killing of Kelly Ann Tinyes as "irrational, inhuman, savage," and told the jurors that he would "not be able to give you a rational explanation for irrational acts. If you try to sit here and comprehend—Is there some reason or justification for doing this to a thirteen-year-old girl?—You'll never come up with one."

Cotter went on to detail the extent of injuries inflicted on Kelly during the violent attack that had ended her life. While the prosecutor spoke Robert Golub feverishly scribbled notes on a legal tablet in front of him, sliding sheets of yellow paper to Marinello; in the rear of the courtroom could be heard the muted weeping of the Tinyes family

"I don't intend to prove that this was premeditated when 'he lured her to the house," Cotter said, "or for whatever reason she went there. But at the time of this attack, he intended to cause death."

As for motive Cotter suggested, "When you have a thirteen-year-old female victim whose clothing is ripped from her body, who is sexually mutilated . . . I think it's fair to assume that this was probably a sexual assault."

He explained that Kelly's throat had been slashed and that her head had puffed out from the swelling caused by the extensive beating she suffered. Cotter held his hands away from his head to demonstrate what he was saying.

The jury would see for itself, he said, that the other three boys in the house at the time had alibis for their actions while Robert Golub had none. Indeed, when he claimed to have been resting on his bed one of the boys had looked into his room and would testify the bed and room were empty.

The prosecutor pointed to Robert and said in a loud voice that he intended to prove beyond a reasonable doubt that "Robert Golub, who sits here wearing a suit and a tie in the courtroom, at the time of his attack, intended to cause the death, and did, in fact, cause the death of Kelly Ann Tinyes." Only Robert had "the means, the motive, and the opportunity" to commit this heinous crime.

When Marinello took his place at the lectern, he voiced his skepticism. Robert was a scapegoat for police officers under intense pressure to make an arrest, any arrest, in the face of so gruesome a crime.

Marinello acknowledged the prosecution had amassed a mountain of physical evidence, but said that it had been contrived to point to his client. "If his guilt in this case could be established by the amount of money that the county of Nassau and the district attorney spent on the investigation, then I'm a loser before I begin this trial. There's no way that I could match the resources that have gone into this case in terms of prosecution.

"But if you read between the lines, the prosecutor is only saying, 'I'm going to produce a lot of witnesses here. I'm going to produce a lot of exhibits and I want you to infer Mr. Golub's guilt.' "

The jury was to understand, Marinello reminded them, that Robert "lives in this house. There is reason to find prints of the whole family in the house. They live there." He assured the jury that "No evidence establishes [Robert's] guilt beyond a reasonable doubt."

Judge Goodman had authorized the hiring of a second defense attorney and Marinello was joined by David Grossman, who was reputedly a specialist in case presentation and cross-examination. He was not to participate in the actual questioning of witnesses, but he was present throughout the trial to assist Marinello.

As the case began, Cotter called Kelly's father, Richard Tinyes, to the stand first. Members of a victim's family usually have little by way of real evidence to offer at such a trial, but they graphically demonstrate the loss a murder has caused and bring to life the deceased who the jurors will only see in photographs. Kelly's father testified that he had lived at 101 Horton Road for twenty-five years and described who lived with him. When Cotter displayed an aerial photograph of the street, Richard identified the name of the family living in every one of the nineteen houses there. He pointed to his own residence, then the location of the Golubs' home.

Wiping tears from his eyes, Kelly's father told the court the clothes his daughter had been wearing the last day of her life, and recounted his final telephone call with his daughter only moments before she left the house against his instructions. Then he described the family's frantic search for his missing daughter that night and the next morning.

During cross-examination Richard told of his conversation with John Jay Golub who denied seeing Kelly for several days and sounded "nervous."

Little Richie Tinyes was called to the stand where he strained to reach the microphone. He testified to receiving the telephone call that had been the reason his older sister left the house. "I'll be right back," he remembered her telling him.

Next Cotter questioned a series of Horton Road neighbors to establish who had entered and exited the Golubs' house and what time each event had taken place. The timing was crucial since it was essential that he leave only Robert with enough unaccounted time to commit the murder and perform the subsequent mutilation and concealment of the body.

Sharon Stonel, who asked that her testimony not be televised, testified to watching Kelly enter the Golubs' house just after three o'clock. Her mother told the jury she had been ironing clothes and had seen Kelly walking up the street at the same time, though she was not able to see the front of the Golubs' house from where she was and did not actually observe Kelly enter the house.

A neighbor who worked at school was driving up to her house when she noticed John Jay and his two friends entering his house at 2:45 P.M. She knew John Jay by sight but specifically recalled him that day because he had been wearing a distinctive jacket with brightly colored sleeves.

A young teenager on the street with a paper route testified he had been in the front yard of his house

folding his papers when he watched John Jay and his
two friends go into the Golubs' house, also at 2:45 P.M.
His mother had driven him on his route and they had
been back at his house by 3:30 P.M. He had spoken to
Sharon Stonel and they were still talking when he saw
John Jay and his friends leave the Golubs' house at 3:45
P.M.

Telephone records were admitted into evidence and a
special agent with the telephone company's security division testified to the sequence and duration of calls
from the Tinyeses' house those crucial days and of the
call from the Golubs' house to the Tinyeses' house on
Friday. It had occurred at 2:50 that afternoon and lasted
precisely 55 seconds.

Then Det. Thomas McVetty took the stand. He recounted the events of that Saturday, his meeting with the
Tinyes family, his questioning of neighbors, and his interview of Robert and John Jay Golub in their home.
Robert was "nervous" as he denied seeing Kelly the previous day and repeatedly looked to his younger brother
as if for assurance when McVetty had asked him simple
questions. "I believe in my notes it indicates that he
looked at his brother back and forth for confirmation of
answers."

McVetty described obtaining the Golubs' signature on
the consent to search form, then the search itself to the
discovery of the body. Cotter handed the detective a
stack of photographs and asked that he identify each
one. These were pictures of the Golubs' house, the main
room of the basement from various viewpoints, the
closet where Kelly was discovered, the sleeping bag, and
then one at which he said, "That's the human foot that
I saw."

Upstairs, while his partner had summoned homicide, McVetty spoke to the Golubs, their daughter, Adele, who had arrived during the search, and John Jay.

"Did you see Robert Golub in the house at the time of the search?" Cotter asked.

"No, he had left."

Patrolman Howard Charney testified to the search in the basement and the discovery of the body. At that time he was looking for a living teenage girl, presumed at the worst to be hiding. He was not prepared for what he discovered in the storage space beneath the stairs. "I noticed a green zippered sleeping bag pushed back under the closet. . . . It appeared to be in a funny position." He turned his flashlight to the bag, reached in and groped about, touching something "which felt like the muscle around a leg or arm." He unzipped the bag and saw "a human leg with dried blood on it."

"I was a little shocked to find that. I backed out from the closet and motioned to Detective McVetty to take a look at what I had found."

Cotter handed Charney a series of photographs which had been taken of the closet before Kelly's body had been removed. Charney examined each in turn and confirmed they were photographs of what he had seen. As he did a muffled sobbing arose from Victoria Tinyes and Linda Player.

The trial took place from Monday through Thursday each week. Friday was reserved so Judge Goodman could handle other matters that were pending on his docket. The courtroom was tightly packed with spectators though no one was permitted to stand. By Monday when the trial resumed, jockeying for the twenty-five seats allocated to the public had already become intense.

The line was well formed by nine each morning. Curiosity-seekers were among them, friends of either family also came, as did the court buffs who made it a practice to attend every sensational murder trial. The wait for a spot in the courtroom lasted more than one hour with no guarantees.

"First come, first serve. This is not a movie theater," the senior court officer explained repeatedly. During lunch breaks friends would hold seats. "You should not be allowed to save a space for someone during lunch," one regular at these trials complained.

Cotter called to the stand one of the three boys who had been playing basketball at the elementary school on Friday, March 3 of the previous year. John Jay and his two friends had shown up uninvited at 3:45 P.M. The game the seven then played lasted about twenty minutes and was not pleasant. The newcomers bickered constantly and sought to intimidate the younger boys.

"Just forget we were here, or next time, there'll be blood on our knuckles," one of them said as they prepared to leave.

"They were all hyper," the boy testified, speaking of John Jay and his friends. " 'I'm so stoned,' " he recalled Earle saying. They had been concerned about the time because they had to meet someone for pizza and asked the hour repeatedly.

Wells had instructed his detectives to determine how long it took to walk from each of the locations the trio claimed to have been that day. Cotter called one of the officers to testify to the findings. It took eight to nine minutes to walk from the elementary school to the pizza parlor, a distance of four-tenths of a mile. It took four minutes to walk from the pizza parlor to the high school, a distance of two-tenths of a mile. It was six minutes from the Golub house to the basketball courts.

Charlie Fox's $4,500 reconstruction of the Golubs' house was now on display in the courtroom and appeared to hold the jurors enthralled. The one-twelfth creation was meticulous in its re-creation. Fox had spent two weeks simply hand painting the exact pattern of the carpet in the basement. The model was accurate to the smallest detail, from bathroom fixtures to the trees and the fence in the yard. The black plastic safety cap from a disposable razor served as the mailbox.

Detective William Steinbeck stepped to the stand the second week of the trial and testified in an authoritative, confident style acquired from years on the witness stand. He was asked to identify over one hundred of the photographs he had taken of the crime scene, starting with the exterior then leading through the house, down the stairs to the basement.

By the use of the photographs which were passed to the jury after each was identified, Cotter led them on a tour of the Golubs' house. Through the yellow wood front door, across the blue carpeted steps to the living room, past the maroon couch covered with piles of clothes and boxes, through the green-plaid wallpapered kitchen, to the other side of the yellow refrigerator, through the doorway, then down the stairs to the cluttered floor below.

The numerous photographs taken of the condition of the basement were quite explicit. Clearly seen were broken bits of glass, boxes, clutter, and refuse all over the floor as well as close-ups of the physical evidence and bloodstains that would shortly be the subject of the trial.

Steinbeck testified he had been present when the sleeping bag containing Kelly's body had been removed from the closet, and he had taken photographs there and of her nude body after the bag was fully unzipped.

"Officer," Cotter asked, "can you tell us what is in this photograph?"

"A view of the deceased in a sleeping bag," Steinbeck replied.

The photographs were passed to the jurors in turn and they had their first view of the murdered teenager. The selection of which photographs of Kelly to use had been carefully made during the pretrial proceedings. The most graphic, indeed the most accurate, photographs of what her killer had done would not be shown so as not to inflame the jury against the accused.

Still, those that were shown were horrifying in their detail. The jurors were grim-faced as they stared at each photograph. When spectators caught a glimpse of a picture, there were gasps and Victoria Tinyes began crying once again. As the testimony continued her quiet tears broke into loud sobs. So disruptive was the sound of the grieving mother that Judge Goodman announced a recess. As court officers swarmed around the two families to keep them separated, Victoria shot a look at the Golubs. When she stood to leave she called Robert "a devil," then his parents "devil people."

After the recess Steinbeck went on to describe what he and his men had removed from the basement: molding, cardboard, paper, and clothing, anything which appeared to have been stained in blood.

The photographic tour resumed as Steinbeck identified pictures taken of the second floor of the Golubs'
house including Robert's unkempt bedroom.

While the photographs of Kelly's body had been star-
tling to the jury and traumatic for the Tinyes family,
they had not been unexpected. This was, after all, a
notorious murder trial. Almost as shocking were the
photographs of the interior of the Golubs' house. Cotter
dwelled at length on Robert's bedroom to counter the
impeccable appearance of the impassive young man sitting beside Marinello with his new, shorter haircut. The
photographs revealed a sheet instead of a door across
the doorway, Robert's bed as unmade, a sweater strewn
across a rocking chair, wall decorations of the backside
of a nude woman, a hunting bow and arrow, snapshots
of weight lifters, and poster-sized photo of rock singer
Stevie Nicks.

Robert had described the day of the killing to detectives as a lazy, typical one for him since he lost his job
and doubtless that accurately captured many of his days.
But the picture painted in the press and by Cotter's case
to the jury created an image closer to the actual life of
the Golub family. The sheet hung across Robert's doorway was a stark reminder that this was not your typical
family.

Fourteen

Steinbeck testified that he had observed what appeared to be a latent print on the molding of the closet where Kelly's body had been discovered. He had administered a field test and determined that the print had been made in blood.

Marinello shot to his feet and objected. "This should have been disclosed to me prior to trial in this case," he told the judge. Cotter informed the court that the existence of the latent print had been disclosed previously.

Marinello didn't agree. "Cotter is playing cute if he's now telling me it was disclosed in [discovery] material a few days ago. For the first time, he discloses the fact that a field test was performed. How can I prepare a defense? . . . That's not fair, Judge."

"I have fully complied with the discovery section," Cotter repeated. "I turned over reports as they were completed by [the police serologist]."

Marinello disagreed, insisting that he had been told by Cotter that "there was no testing done because it would have destroyed this print" which was a "major piece of evidence . . . a critical piece of evidence against the defendant." He asked Judge Goodman to wipe out the testimony concerning the field test, or he intended to move for a mistrial. For now the court instructed the attorneys to proceed while he considered the objection which he subsequently denied.

Steinbeck testified to other areas in the basement where blood had been located, including in and around the attaché cases that contained Kelly's clothing, and on the basement carpet.

Now Steinbeck was subjected to a grueling two-hour cross-examination by Marinello, who repeatedly challenged the competency of his evidence gathering.

"Didn't you take that attaché case and put it right on top of that [blood]stain?" Marinello asked.

"No, sir," Steinbeck replied.

"Sure of that?"

"Yes, sir."

Marinello had the officer repeat how disheveled and cluttered the Golubs' basement had been and that it would be difficult to move around without upsetting some key bit of evidence. Repeatedly he asked Steinbeck whether "the integrity of the crime scene was disturbed?"

"There is always the chance of losing something," Steinbeck acknowledged at one point, "but you learn through experience you have to be careful."

Next Cotter summoned sixteen-year-old Mick Donnell to the stand. With bright red hair, dressed in tweed and a dress shirt with a tie, the boy approached the witness stand with his hands clasped before him as if he were about to receive the Eucharist.

The boy earnestly described the events of Friday, March 3, one year before, when he, Earle, and John Jay had gone upstairs to smoke marijuana. The stereo was so loud it had not been possible to hear anything in the house.

"We were play-fighting around," he said. "We were laughing. We were stoned."

"Had Kelly Tinyes ever been mentioned up to this time?" Cotter asked him.

"No, sir."

Did the boys ever go into the basement that day? "No, we didn't," Donnell replied. And most importantly, he testified that at no time was any one of the three ever out of the sight of the other two for more than a few seconds.

Under cross-examination the teenager outlined his drug use, even naming those who supplied him with marijuana, LSD, and mescaline. Marinello asked, "Weren't you in sort of a fog during that time while you were using those substances? Can you really be sure about what you were talking about when you were stoned?"

The boy said, yes, he could be certain of his memory. He had not started using the heavier drugs until the summer after Kelly was murdered. He was now in a drug rehabilitation center out of state.

On Friday, February 23, the trial was interrupted during the testimony of one of the officers describing the state of affairs when he first arrived at the Golubs' house. Security officers suddenly flooded the room creating a stir as one whispered into Judge Goodman's ear. He summoned Cotter and Marinello to the bench and seconds later the jury was ushered from the courtroom. Only then did the judge announce that there had been a bomb threat and everyone was to clear the courthouse while a search was conducted of the building. That proved futile and an hour later the trial resumed with the detective's description of Robert Golub's interrogation. Most significantly he reported that Robert had insisted repeatedly that he had not been in the basement the previous day. He said he had been asleep in his room from the time his brother and friends were upstairs until he was awakened early that evening.

When Robert's fingerprints were being taken the detective testified, "I noticed on his right hand several small cuts or lacerations. He had two cuts on the right thumb finger, in the middle finger. There was another small cut on the top of that finger. Above his pinkie there was a small cut in the knuckle area.

"I asked Mr. Golub how he had gotten those cuts on his hand. He told me he was a weight lifter, that he was into competitive weight lifting and that he had probably gotten the cuts from adjusting the weight-lifting bar." During his testimony the detective identified photographs taken of Robert's hands and these were now placed into evidence.

Under Marinello's cross-examination the detective described a conversation Robert told him he had the day Kelly's body was discovered in his house. "He told me that his brother John had come up to his room and told him that there were some detectives downstairs that wanted to talk to him and that when he talked to them to tell the police I was playing Nintendo and don't say anything about smoking."

Dr. Arlene Colon, the forensic serologist for the county Medical Examiner's Office who had attended the autopsy, was called to the stand and testified as to the results of tests she had performed.

Colon, youthful in appearance with bangs and glasses,

testified that while no semen had been detected on Kelly's body, considerable evidence of saliva was present. There were weak reactions for semen on one shirt found near the body.

She further testified that cuts had been found on the young girl's body, that her clothing had been ripped from her, and that tufts of hair were torn from her head. The turtleneck sweater which had been ripped apart in pulling it from Kelly had tested positive for both Kelly's own blood and for saliva.

The bayonet was admitted into evidence and handed to her. "I found positive indications of blood along the blade, from the tip to the hilt on both sides," she said. A court attendant displayed the weapon for the jury, walking slowly up and down the two lines, so each juror could examine the knife as Colon testified.

During cross-examination the serologist agreed with Marinello that the weak tests for semen suggested the stain was at least several days old. She also testified that the saliva had characteristics consistent with both Kelly's and Robert's blood types and she could not say from whom it had come.

Colon had not swabbed appropriate areas to test for rust. Later tests proved negative.

Most of the cuts performed on Kelly's body were not consistent with the bayonet, she testified, and she had concluded that it was not the primary instrument used.

The body had so much blood on it that it was carefully examined for prints but none were found. An apparent latent print was detected on one of the girl's sneakers, but it proved too smudged to be of use.

A sharp exchange occurred when the defense attorney criticized the conduct of the autopsy concerning the saliva found on Kelly's body. Colon had testified that most of it was washed away and not enough remained for specific classifying. "I did not note the bite marks because the body was so smeared with blood."

Marinello demanded to know how "an important piece of information" could just be "washed away."

"It's an unfortunate thing that it was not noted in the beginning," Colon replied.

During this testimony Robert turned and smiled weakly at his parents, who were sitting not far behind him. One of the Tinyes family shouted, "Turn around!" Robert complied.

Judge Goodman admonished the spectators against further outbursts, but when Colon's testimony was concluding there were more shouts from the Tinyes family, including one of "animal" which was directed at Robert.

As the graphic testimony mounted Victoria Tinyes, wearing dark sunglasses, found it increasingly difficult to remain in her seat. Three times while Colon spoke she bolted from her place and loudly exited the courtroom in the midst of livid testimony. Each time she stood tellingly in front of her chair before leaving the courtroom, glaring at the Golub family sitting across the aisle.

Richard Tinyes commented during a break, "I don't think any parent would want to listen to this. . . . It's hard to live through this all over again."

During the lunch break a shouting match erupted in the hallway as the Tinyes family and supporters cursed and screamed at the Golubs. This time they shouted back.

"We have every right to attend his trial," an angry

John Golub said. "If it was their son and they weren't here, there would be something wrong with them. We are trying to ignore them but they make it very difficult." Again he complained of the daily harassment he and his family faced on Horton Road.

"Why don't they leave us alone," his daughter Adele said, "and just let the trial be the issue?"

Richard Tinyes responded. "They are harassing us by just being at the trial. Maybe they ought to move away."

"Far, far away," Victoria added.

Marinello found these constant courtroom interruptions to be disruptive of the process. Several times he had difficulty with cross-examination of witnesses because spectators were making noises behind him. Judge Goodman did not seem to hear them; though the judge cautioned for silence when Marinello called it to his attention, the disruptive noise would resume.

In addition, Marinello was troubled by the presence of the Tinyes family and their supporters. He did not object to those who had been wronged in a crime attending the trial; he did object to the constant shouts and the conspicuous exiting. This all had to have an impact on the jury which was present for much of it. The situation was aggravated by the fact that the Tinyes family sat behind the defense which was on the side of the courtroom closest to the jury.

Marinello was finding the trial exhausting. His practice consisted primarily of criminal cases and most of his other work had been farmed out to other lawyers. He was working nonstop, seven days a week on this case. His personal situation was exacerbated by the fact that he was receiving death threats. His children had also been threatened at school as well and more than once had to be removed for their safety. He was particularly bothered because his daughter was thirteen years old, the same age Kelly had been, and made an ideal target for some wacko.

The next day Judge Goodman had assigned two more court security officers expressly to escort the Golub family.

Wayne Birdsall was called and testified that he had been performing serology work now as a specialist for over twelve years. With Cotter asking the questions the detective testified that the Saturday Kelly's body had been discovered had been a day off for him. He had received the summons to report to the Golubs' residence at his home and arrived on Horton Road just after four in the afternoon. He had begun with a careful examination of the exterior of the house, searching methodically for signs of blood. He had checked the sidewalks, streets, neighboring lawns, driveways, and the backyard.

As darkness came over the street he moved to the interior of the house, beginning his search in the living and dining rooms, then the kitchen. The first blood he spotted was on the carpet as he entered the basement at the bottom of the stairs. In the closet under the stairs he found a large puddle of blood and curtains saturated with blood. He observed bloodstains on the paneling of the walls and on the molding.

At the rear of the basement Birdsall uncovered bloodstains on the walls, three large stains on the floor, and more on the carpet. He found blood on the doorknob of the room where he ultimately determined Kelly had been killed, more blood on two of the attaché cases, and still more blood on clothes found inside three of the cases.

Once he identified where he had found blood, Birdsall then testified to administering the tests he used to classify each stain. To assist the jury Birdsall worked from a chart to which he made periodic reference. He described the various ways he could type the blood and the problems the quantity of blood could present in preventing certain tests since some blood was consumed in all testing. He testified to the process he had used to eliminate the Golubs, John Jay, Donnell, and Earle. The only matches he did make were consistent with either Kelly or Robert.

Cotter presented to Birdsall various articles of clothing. He gave the detective Kelly's sneakers which he said bore traces of blood consistent with the girl's. Then Cotter handed him her white silk panties with lace around the waist, and again it contained blood consistent with Kelly's. Birdsall took Kelly's cardigan sweater which was heavily stained with blood. Only one of the five buttons was still on it. The other four buttons had been found on the floor of the basement where they had fallen after the sweater was ripped apart. This sweater, and the buttons, all contained blood consistent with the teenager's.

Birdsall handled Kelly's clothes in a manner that suggested sensitivity to the fact that they belonged to a person and were not simply pieces of abstract evidence.

For several days now Robert Golub had become increasingly animated. The first two weeks of the trial, it had seemed that he was in search of something useful to do, and had constantly shuffled and rearranged the papers in front of him. From time to time he leaned to Marinello to whisper and a moment later would be handed a breath mint. When the chart of blood samples had been displayed, Robert had maneuvered himself to observe it clearly.

The manner of presenting physical evidence in a criminal trial is to offer it, hand it to the defense, then present it to the witness. This had been followed with the photographs the first and second weeks of testimony, and it appeared that Robert had lingered a fraction of a second longer over the pictures of the "death room" than he had the others.

Birdsall was given a blue tablecloth to identify and treated it more cavalierly than he had the articles of clothing that had come from the victim.

The tablecloth, Birdsall said, contained two types of blood. One consistent with Kelly, the other consistent with Robert.

Cotter asked if the stain "was consistent with a mixed stain being applied" at the same time.

"I would think so," Birdsall answered.

Referring to a stain of blood on the inside of Kelly's leather jacket, Cotter asked, "Is that blood consistent with the defendant's blood in this case?"

"Yes."

Handed tissue paper, "Is that consistent with anyone else on that chart?"

"Yes, Robert Golub."

Finally, Cotter asked if it was correct that the odds of "a stranger walking" into the Golubs' house and possessing the identical blood identifiers as Robert Golub was a thousand to one.

"Correct," Birdsall replied.

The testimony had been riveting and gone very much against Robert Golub, yet the young man had never before appeared so confident or been so active. He spoke frequently with Marinello and smiled a great deal, once stifling a yawn at a key point of the testimony.

During that day's lunch break a friend of the Tinyes family thrust a bumper sticker with an obscenity on it at Elizabeth Golub and screamed to her companions, "I hate her! I hate her!" Officers pulled the woman away as she told those she was with, "I just wanted to show them how much I disliked them."

Fifteen

Birdsall was on the stand for three days and was relentless in his presentation. One by one he identified repeated pieces of evidence on which he had found blood: glass, an old family photograph, a T-shirt, and the sleeping bag. He had found evidence nearly everywhere he turned, and the cumulative effect of his testimony was to bring home the full magnitude of the violent death Kelly Ann Tinyes had suffered.

"I finally had to stay away," Richard Tinyes said. "It's horrifying to sit there and listen to it all." For this day he tried to work.

On the third day of Birdsall's testimony, Marinello began what would become a six-and-a-half-hour cross-examination. By focusing on just one of several identifiers for which Birdsall had tested, Marinello attempted to suggest that the blood samples could have come from any of several persons. Referring to one of the attaché cases, the attorney asked that since the PGM was 2+ could it have come from Elizabeth Golub, John Jay, or Robert. There was no way to tell. Birdsall agreed.

"Something happened between March ninth and March tenth when you tested stains one through twenty-two and when you did stain twenty-three where you found

PGM with two plus and one plus one, didn't it?" Marinello asked.

"What do you mean, 'Something happened'?"

"Well, you came into possession of blood samples from the defendant. You were given samples of defendant's blood between the time you did twenty-two and the time you did twenty-three, right?"

"March fourteenth," Birdsall answered, meaning the day he received Robert Golub's blood sample. He explained that he had not performed any of the additional tests until he knew which EAPs he was searching for. He did not have enough blood in all his samples to run the test for every possible EAP.

Marinello's cross-examination of Birdsall was frequently quite heated. He suggested at one point that Birdsall's testimony was often nothing more than a "judgment call," a phrase he used repeatedly.

Reading the bands produced by the testing was a "judgment call" Marinello insisted, and asking other police serologists to review the results for confirmation was like showing the results "to another police officer."

Birdsall took exception. "I'm asking a scientist to make that decision."

The jurors followed the numerous exchanges intently.

Marinello suggested the equipment Birdsall had used must have been defective. Birdsall disagreed, but acknowledged he did not know the last time it had been checked.

During the afternoon Marinello turned to tests Birdsall had performed on ten blood samples. One of the small samples was consistent with both Kelly and Earle.

"You don't know whether that is in fact the blood of Kelly Ann Tinyes or Chris Earle?"

"The sample size wouldn't allow [further testing]," Birdsall answered.

Robert seemed pleased with the questioning and during a recess he turned, smiled at his parents, and flashed them the victory sign.

When Birdsall concluded his testimony later that afternoon, the trial had completed its third full week and the exhausted court personnel and lawyers were grateful when Judge Goodman scheduled the first full workday off.

Before lunch that day the Golubs met again with reporters. They repeated that they did not know what happened that day in their basement, though they were certain that neither of their sons had anything to do with the murder.

"Robert was a good boy," his mother said. "He had two, three paper routes as a kid. . . . There is no doubt in my mind . . . I haven't got the faintest, faintest . . . in my faintest imagination, I can't believe he did it."

Robert, his parents said, was a fastidious young man. "He did not like to get his hands dirty."

The couple took exception to their house being portrayed in the media as junk-filled. "They keep saying junk. You see, my wife is a collector. She can't pass up a bargain."

They rarely went into the basement. "I have a bad leg," John Golub explained. His wife had been injured previously in a car accident and had difficulty getting around as well.

What is it like, they were asked, to live in a house where a murder occurred?

"Everybody asks me that question," Elizabeth said. "But Kelly has never affected me once, as far as my conscience. I can live with myself." If she really thought her son was responsible she might feel different.

The unfolding trial had produced still another reason for the families on Horton Road to be angry with the Golubs. Just as the facade of their house had been neat and orderly, just as it seemed to match the rest of the houses on the street, disclosures had revealed an interior and a family in diametric contrast. It had been like a public unmasking and neighbors still were not certain what other terrible secrets the family held. So, too, had they witnessed the unmasking of Robert, the unveiling of an inner self in absolute contrast to his pleasing surface appearance.

For months now Wells had watched the incredible resources of modern forensic science at play in this one murder case. Before it began he had scarcely known that certain of the procedures existed. He thought back over some of his unsolved homicides and was troubled to conclude that there were those of them that he could have solved if the same commitment of resources had taken place.

The first of the crucial testimony, and what would prove to be the climax of the trial, began when it resumed on March 5, one year from the day that would have been Kelly's fourteenth birthday. That weekend the girl's friends had launched fifty helium-filled balloons into the sky over Valley Stream as the crowd shouted, "Happy birthday, Kelly."

For months it had been apparent that the most significant evidence the People possessed would be the results of the highly source-specific DNA testing. Marinello had tried repeatedly to bar the evidence from the trial during the fall's protracted hearings, but Judge Goodman had ruled the DNA results would be admitted.

Until now there had been an air of uncertainty about the trial. So many witnesses had testified to so little, and certainly to nothing that indicated the accused young man was a murderer. It was as if the prosecution was punching at air. Even Birdsall's damning testimony had left at least some room for doubt.

A precise, clear-speaking, attractive woman in her early thirties with short, dark hair, Lorah McNally had testified a number of times previously. When the DNA tests had been performed, she was Lifecodes's forensic laboratory supervisor and was now assistant director of Forensic Research. Much of the work Lifecodes performed was intended for court and she had participated in a two-day training course on how to conduct herself on the witness stand. What she had learned was to speak in a clear voice, at a level where the common man could comprehend what she was saying, and to address the jury because it was to whom her testimony was directed.

DNA testing was barely a decade old and had been making its appearance in criminal trials for only the last two years. Though it had received most of its initial criminal publicity as a prosecutor's tool, DNA results were a two-edged sword. Lifecodes's first participation in a criminal matter had occurred two years earlier when its findings led to the release of two convicted rapists.

Cotter began by having McNally deliver a primer on DNA. The center of every cell, she said, is a nucleus, and it is from that nucleus that DNA is extracted. The structure of DNA is organized into chromosomes of which twenty-three pairs are present inside each nucleus. Basically DNA is like two pieces of string that are wound around each other and are tightly compacted into chromosome structures. DNA is double-stranded, she testified, and should be thought of as a ladder with complementary strands of chromosomes on each side of the ladder. Each side of the ladder is precisely and unerringly matched to the other.

In human blood the nucleus is found in white blood cells; the red cells have no nucleus. Twenty-three of the human chromosomes come from the father and twenty-three from the mother. As a result members of the same family have DNA similar to one another though still identifiable as distinct.

Cotter displayed a chart to which McNally pointed and each member of the jury had been given a copy of the chart to follow along. Judge Goodman appeared fascinated by the testimony and hung on McNally's every word.

There were, she explained, seven steps in determining the DNA pattern of any individual. First, the DNA must be isolated from the particular biological material in which it was contained, in this case, the blood samples the police had given her. Then the cells were broken open and the DNA in the nucleus extracted.

The second step was to purify the DNA by eliminating any protein, excess lipids, fats, and other material that is not needed. Once the DNA was isolated it appeared as long strands. To conduct the analysis it was necessary to fragment, or cut, the DNA with an enzyme. This slices the ladder, as it were, into several thousand pieces, each with the matching chromosome still in place.

These pieces were now arranged according to size by electrophoresis. The pieces were placed on a gel and the current was administered. DNA has a slightly negative charge so there is movement toward the positive electrode and the distance of the movement was determined by the size of the piece.

Next the DNA fragments were sorted according to size and separated into single strands of chromosomes. These were then transferred to a nylon membrane which was easier to handle than the gel. A probe consisting of a known piece of DNA was now added so it was possible to visualize the results. The single chromosomes stick to the probe according to their genetic predisposition, in a consistent and predictable manner.

The final step was to wash the excess probe away, then put X-ray film on top of the membrane. The film was exposed and the visual marker contained in the probe produced a band wherever the probe stuck to a chromosome.

"Now the band, or the known area of DNA, that's been located on the fragments on the membrane, how does that relate in relation to one sample of blood versus another sample?" Cotter asked.

"What you're going to see is a pattern. What you do is . . . to compare first of all the number of bands that are observed, and second, the position of the bands, so that if you have a known sample you look at the position of those two bands of the sample, you compare it to an unknown and you make a determination whether or not these two bands match or do not match."

As it applied in this case, each sample had produced a series of bands which very much resembled an abacus. These were matched to Kelly Ann Tinyes's known blood and by comparison could determine if the sample was hers. The same applied to Robert Golub. McNally could match the bands produced from a tested sample to the bands produced from the blood drawn from him. A match meant it was his blood pattern in the sample, a sample which had been taken from the scene of the murder.

Cotter asked whether the "millions" of chemical pairings in DNA allowed "for the DNA in individuals to be almost unique in every individual in the world."

"That's right," she said. Only identical twins possessed the same DNA. Cotter now directed McNally's testimony to the case at hand. "How different does that process [you just described] differ from the forensic testing you did in this case on the attaché cases?"

"The difference is really step number one. You don't necessarily start with a blood sample that is in a tube. You may start with a bloodstain or a semen stain or a tissue cell."

"For comparison to that you also receive blood samples from the police department in this particular case?"

"Yes. . . . Whether blood comes from a vial of blood or came from a stain I extracted from the attaché cases, this is the beginning of testing. . . . You would take a small amount of that sample and you would add a solution which basically makes the cells rupture and releases the DNA so that it is now available."

Cotter led McNally through the specific steps her lab

had followed in testing the samples in this case, emphasizing the procedures designed to ensure accuracy. In all such tests two control marker lanes with known results were run along with the sample.

McNally testified that she had received two attaché cases from Birdsall in mid-March the previous year along with five other samples of blood. These were from Robert, John Jay, Elizabeth, and John Golub, and also from Kelly Ann Tinyes.

She observed a large stain on the lid of one of the attaché cases. Other stains on the top of the cases appeared as smears or even as a fine film. Both cases had two stains on the bottom. She designated the stains on top of the two attaché cases with blood as evidence A and the three stains located on the bottom as evidence B.

On August 29, 1989, she had received blood samples drawn from Donnell and Earle to assist in the matching.

"What exactly did you do to remove stains on the outside of the cases for testing?" Cotter asked.

"I took a Q-Tips swab, moistened it, swabbed off the area that had stain. I then processed the swab as a sample." To gather enough material for DNA testing she combined both A samples on top of the attaché cases.

Five probes can be used in DNA testing and in this case Lifecodes utilized each in succession. Again McNally referred to her chart as she explained that samples could be exposed to X rays for up to three days and that not all bands were of the same darkness. The intensity of the band was directly related to the amount or concentration of DNA contained in the sample.

"Can you take the top probe and tell us what the findings are and what they reflect as to what was found

in the evidence samples and who might have contributed
that DNA?" Cotter asked.

McNally answered that this probe did not eliminate
Robert or John Jay Golub, but it did exclude their
mother. Such a finding was not unusual given that the
two brothers had the same parents.

Cotter asked if the results excluded Kelly Ann Tinyes,
and McNally answered, "That's correct."

"Knowing that both Robert and John Jay had that
band found in evidence A, can you go to the second
probe and tell us what the results were with respect to
the testing?"

"The pattern that we obtained from John Jay Golub
contained four bands and when you're looking at these
patterns the two things one wants to focus on is the
number of bands and the position of the bands with
respect as to how they fall from top to bottom. So that
in this particular case this four-banded pattern obtained
from the blood sample labeled John Jay Golub does not
match the three-banded pattern obtained from the evidence from the bloodstain labeled [evidence] A from
the top of the briefcases."

She explained that John Jay's four bands did not line
up with the three-banded pattern found from the stain
in evidence A. Further, the bands did not match John
or Elizabeth Golub, or for that matter, either Donnell
or Earle.

"Can you tell what the results of Robert's DNA re-
veal with respect to evidence stain A?"

"With the second probe system the print that came
from the blood labeled Robert matched the print obtained from the DNA isolated from the evidence . . .
Then I discovered this interesting comparison," McNally

said. She pointed to several faded points on the bar of Robert's blood. "These match precisely with that of the victim's." She paused, then Cotter asked what was the significance.

"It means I am reading two codes from one specimen. In other words, the blood of Robert Golub and Kelly Tinyes is comingled," she said.

Successive probes were run and "the visual pattern of DNA resulting remained consistent with the visual pattern and sizing of the blood sample of Robert . . . All predominate bands on evidence A are consistent with DNA bands of Robert."

After running four probes McNally had reached the conclusion "that the DNA isolated from the bloodstain labeled A from the two tops of the briefcases matched the pattern obtained from the blood labeled Robert Golub. It also contained additional bands that were consistent with the bands obtained from the victim's sample."

In other words, Robert's bands were intermixed with bands that revealed some of the blood had come from Kelly Ann Tinyes. There was no doubt that both their blood was present on top of the two attaché cases.

Lifecodes' more sophisticated procedures had reached two conclusions the police laboratory had not been able to achieve. Displaying the bar codes for the jury, McNally pointed to each matching point. They clearly demonstrated that the blood found in the basement could not have belonged to John Jay or to his parents or friends for that matter. There was not even a close comparison. That alone would have been enough to point an accusing finger at Robert, but then McNally compared his code and the points of match were obvious. There was no question blood found in the basement was his, as there was no question the other blood was Kelly's.

In fact, she explained, in two places, one on the top of the attaché case where the killer had pressed to close the case and the other on the blue tablecloth where the glass had sliced through to cut his hand, Robert's and Kelly's blood was intermixed. For someone who claimed he had not seen Kelly or even been in the basement for two weeks prior to her murder, this was devastating in its impact.

Cotter concluded his questioning of McNally by asking, "What is the percent of population that would have all the bands contained in those five probes [of Robert Golub]?"

"The likelihood of seeing that pattern in the random population is one in seven hundred seven million," McNally answered.

Sixteen

Nolan had made a point to stay away from the trial which had now entered its fourth week. He wanted very much to attend, especially to listen to McNally's testimony, but he knew it was bad form for the chief of homicide to show a disproportionate interest in any single case. His presence would have "sent the wrong message." This would only play into Marinello's claim that his detectives, desperate to pin this despicable murder on someone, anyone, had gone out of their way to place the blame on Robert Golub. As a result Nolan had learned of the progress of the trial from news reports, returning police witnesses, and cryptic conversations with Wells, who had little time to talk out of the courtroom. Cotter had him and Pierce running last-minute errands whenever court was not in session.

Hearing of McNally's testimony Nolan decided that the lengthy questioning of Robert had not been such a waste after all. He had claimed repeatedly that he had not seen Kelly and had not been in the basement the day of or after her murder. His denials had backed him into a corner and gave him no maneuvering room at all. An innocent man would not have told lies, and the jury could surely not help but see the point.

* * *

Marinello began his cross-examination of McNally by reminding jurors that Lifecodes was a for-profit company and that McNally was a witness paid by the State of New York. Lifecodes was one of only two companies doing criminal forensic work and, he said to McNally, "there was a rush to get into this kind of business because a lot of money would be made in DNA forensic testing, but Lifecodes really had no experience when they set up this laboratory."

"No, I wouldn't say that was a fair statement." Lifecodes had done work since 1982 in paternity cases using DNA testing.

"You are certainly aware, as a salaried employee, that there is a great deal of dissension in the scientific community in this country concerning the validity of DNA analysis techniques as they are presently being used, are you not?"

"No, I'm not."

Marinello attacked McNally for having mixed samples from the top of the two attaché cases. "Does that not violate the first cardinal rule when you're dealing with samples before you do an analysis?"

"No," McNally answered. She had combined the samples in order to obtain enough blood to test and in her testimony had clearly stated that the blood had matched samples from both Kelly and Robert.

Ignoring earlier testimony that the blood found on the attaché cases had been fresh, Marinello asked, "Isn't it a fact that a sample could have been on that briefcase months and weeks before?"

McNally's test did nothing to establish the age of the samples tested. "That's possible," she said.

Moving on, Marinello asked, "When you talk about the matches you're not saying with a reasonable degree of certainty the blood of one particular individual matches the blood from an evidence sample, are you?"

"What we are saying is the DNA pattern obtained in a blood sample does or does not match a DNA pattern obtained in the evidence sample."

"There is no known technique, be it DNA analysis or genetic marker analysis from blood samples, that can tell you that blood on an evidence sample is, in fact, blood from a particular individual, correct?"

"That's right. You're looking at that particular pattern and determining the frequency of that pattern in the population."

Next Marinello attacked the number of probes used and questioned the accuracy of Lifecodes's written report. McNally responded to each of his questions and proved herself to be a tough witness. She exhibited no nervousness and was unhesitating in her replies. She remained composed and continued to direct her answers to the jury.

Testimony and cross-examination of McNally proceeded through three grueling and dramatic days while outside a winter storm raged. The start of one day of her testimony was delayed because jurors arrived late on account of snow-covered roads, and another day's testimony was concluded early so jurors could reach home before dark.

When McNally stepped down upon the conclusion of her testimony, there was the sense the People had surmounted its burden. What remained was for Robert to respond, if he dared.

Cotter had more testimony, however, and now turned to other, though less precise, forensic evidence which pointed a guilty finger at Robert Golub. A single, nine-inch strand of hair had been found in Robert's bedding that testing suggested belonged to Kelly. Wells believed the strand had been inadvertently carried by Robert back to his room on his clothing or nude body after he had killed Kelly in the basement.

Marinello objected to Cotter's calling the investigator-technician who had conducted the examination of the strand of hair because it was scientifically inexact. Cotter acknowledged that such a comparison "is not as conclusive as fingerprints," but said his witness would testify to this strand's microscopic similarity to Kelly Ann Tinyes's hair "in thirty different areas." Judge Goodman allowed the testimony.

Officer Vito Schiraldi had worked in the Nassau Crime Lab for three and a half years handling and analyzing trace evidence recovered from crime scenes. This was only the second time he had testified and his nervousness was evident.

Schiraldi said that the strand located in Robert's bed was superficially comparable to the victim's hair. He had microscopically enlarged the hair ten times and examined its pigmentation, cortex, medulla, and others of the thirty characteristics that exist in human hair. Schiraldi had compared this sample to samples of hair taken from the others known to have been in the house at the time, including Robert Golub, and found it was not consistent with any of them.

The strand of hair at issue was darkish brown and proceeded in color to auburn, then to reddish at midshaft and finally blondish-light brown toward the tip. This was a natural progression of pigmentation and was not the result of chemical interaction. Further, the strand's cortex had a ruddy texture to it and scales on the cuticle which were uplifted in a pattern consistent with someone who brushed their hair routinely several times a day, creating a ruddy, brittle texture. This was precisely what he discovered when he examined a strand of hair taken from Kelly Ann Tinyes.

Based on his examination Schiraldi concluded that the strand "could have" come from Kelly. It was not possible to say that the hair was actually from the victim. Such analysis more easily eliminated persons than it accurately identified them.

Marinello made the point repeatedly that it was not possible for Schiraldi to say the hair came from the deceased. The officer acknowledged the point. Then Marinello inexplicably asked for his opinion about the hair.

"My opinion?"

"Right."

"In my opinion it originated from the deceased, but my science doesn't allow me to say that."

Marinello attempted to create doubt about the origin of the single strand since Schiraldi had not collected the bedding from the Golubs' house personally. A protracted examination took place over whether or not pubic hair was body hair and why body hair found in the bedding had not been tested. "Again," Schiraldi said, "let me explain that to find someone's own hair in their own house, as you have hair in your house, has really no meaning in my eyes, in a forensic scientist's eyes, as having any evidentiary value. Having a defendant's hair on the victim's body, that is important. Having the victim, who usually is not [living at] the scene of the crime, having their hair at the scene of the crime ties them in with the scene of the crime . . ."

After suggesting the crime scene might have been contaminated, Marinello concluded his cross-examination by asking, "Is there any way to tell by microscopically looking at a particular hair what time a hair was left there?"

"No, but there are several indications that it—there was no dirt adhering to it and that would leave you to believe it was clean. There was no damage to the cuticle and this would lead you to believe it was deposited in the recent past."

The next day, March 8, Cotter called Chris Earle to the stand. Earle testified to many of the same events Donnell had covered earlier. He had been at the Golubs' house that day, had witnessed and heard nothing. The last time he had seen Robert Golub was when he poked his head into the bedroom where the three of them were smoking marijuana and declined a proffered marijuana cigarette from John Jay.

As the boys were leaving to go downstairs, Earle had put his head through the sheet that passed for a door to Robert's room. He observed a rocking chair sitting on top of the bed and a vacuum cleaner on the floor.

"Did you ever see Robert in that bed?" Cotter asked.

"No."

A detective had previously testified that Robert told him that after seeing his brother and two friends he had gone to his room then slept. He had remained in his room until early that evening. This testimony was a direct contradiction.

Earle was followed by police officer Ron Crowe, and Wells braced himself for where he knew this would be leading.

Cotter began by asking Crowe to explain to the jury what a latent print was. Crowe explained a latent print was a chance impression left by the friction ridge areas of the skin of the fingers, palms of hands, or the soles of feet. It was left behind by perspiration, greases, oils, or fluids that are present on the skin when it comes in contact with a surface. The print was not always visible to the naked eye and has to be processed with powders or chemicals to be seen.

Friction skin, the kind that leaves prints, has high and low areas and recognizable, distinctive patterns, Crowe said. Ridges on the skin scroll, ended, doubled back on themselves in patterns that were unique to that person.

"Is there a difference in pattern that you see on fingers versus a pattern that might appear on the palm portion of the hand?" Cotter asked.

"In your fingers they normally form patterns and there are three basic types. There is a loop which appears where the ridges come up, flow in one direction and flow back into the same direction. The second type of pattern that you might have is called a whorl, in which it appears that the ridges whorl around in a circular formation. The third type is an arch in which the ridges appear to rise and drop down and go out of the other portion of your finger.

"These are present mostly in just your fingers. Once you get out of your fingers into your palms, most of these areas are made up of straight lines or slightly curving lines.

"The characteristics that are within the ridge structure is unique. The two basic fundamentals of fingerprints are that the friction ridge areas of the skin are formed before birth and they remain unchanged in their detail until after death when they are destroyed through decomposition. And that the detail or characteristic layout of the friction skin is never duplicated on the body of that same person anywhere or on the body of any other person."

Crowe explained that many factors contributed to a person's ability to leave a fingerprint. Hot days when sweat was produced were more conducive to leaving a print, while a recently washed hand was unlikely to leave any imprint. The type of surface made a difference as well as did the way in which the friction skin had come in contact with the surface.

"We consider a latent impression as an impression that has enough ridge detail or characteristics in it to make an identification. If it does not have sufficient ridge detail in it to make an identification, it is called a smudge."

Cotter handed Crowe a photograph identified as People's exhibit number 645. It was a picture of the latent print from the molding of the closet where Kelly had been discovered. "In this photograph," Crowe testified, "there was a substance on the friction skin when it touched the molding." Crowe had not tested the substance so he could not say it was blood. Another officer had already done that. "An inked impression as opposed to a latent impression is a deliberate recording of the friction ridge areas of the skin using printer's ink or an inking medium and recording surface, normally a fingerprint card. It is deliberate as opposed to a chance impression of the friction skin."

Crowe explained how officers take fingerprints, then identified the palmprint impression taken from Robert Golub and the actual molding from which the photograph had been taken.

When he began his examination of the latent print he also had the fingerprints of the entire Golub family, Donnell, Earle, Paul Zerella, and of the victim.

He observed that the latent print was composed primarily of straight lines so he went to each of the fingerprint cards and searched them out for similar areas. He found it very difficult to find a starting point for him to begin a detail examination on any of the cards. "There are no pattern types to look for that might key you into a certain finger or area that you are looking for."

"Did there come a time when you found any ridge characteristics that you felt was a comfortable starting point? In other words, an area that had certain distinct characteristics that you try to match as a starting point in the inked impressions?" Cotter asked.

"Yes, there did."

"Did there come a time you had occasion to examine the fingerprint card or palm impression of the defendant in this case, Robert Golub?"

"Yes, there was."

"Did you have occasion to find a match with respect

to the starting point that you had in the latent . . . in Mr. Golub's palmprint?"

"Yes, I did."

"Which of the palmprints did you find that starting point?"

"In the left palm."

"Officer Crowe, have you arrived at an opinion with respect to the identification of the individual that left that latent impression on the molding depicted in the crime-scene photograph?"

"The latent impression that was left on the molding was made by the left palm of Robert Golub."

A large reproduction of the photograph of the latent print found on the molding and of the similar area on Robert Golub's palmprint was now displayed for comparison. First it was shown to Marinello. Robert scooted his chair beside his lawyer. He pointed to places on the chart as he whispered to his lawyer. But mostly his eyes shot back and forth from his own print to the one found with Kelly's body.

Now the chart was displayed for the jury to see. The chart had red lines matching identical points on each print with corresponding numbers. Crowe stepped down from the witness stand and with a pointer was led by Cotter to each of the matching points on the two sets of prints. As he began a disturbance broke out among the spectators and Marinello objected to the court. Judge Goodman instructed those responsible to leave and two women noisily exited the courtroom, one of whom sneered at Robert as she passed closest to him.

As Crowe's testimony relating to the chart resumed, Robert was permitted to stand beside the jurors so he could see where Crowe was indicating with his pointer.

"All the characteristics that are present in this latent impression must match up to the corresponding characters that are in this rolled [inked] impression or an identification cannot be made." Crowe located the points of similarity between the latent print taken from the scene of the murder with those of the print taken from Robert at the police station. "Using these ten characteristics," those indicated by red lines, "the remaining thirteen characteristics that I have plotted throughout this latent," marked by red dots, "I compared all twenty-three characteristics that are present in this inked impression, and it is my conclusion that the latent impression on the molding was left by the left palm of Robert Golub. . . . Once the identification is made it can be no one else."

Back on the witness stand Crowe identified a second piece of molding and two pieces of glass, then testified the prints on them were smudged and not identifiable. A small portion of a print was detected on the zipper of the sleeping bag in which Kelly had been stuffed, but there were not enough point characteristics to identify the print.

A print found on a large weighing scale proved to be John Golub's and a palm impression found on the outer edge of a table was not identifiable. Crowe could not say how long either print had been present.

Crowe's testimony resumed the following Monday with cross-examination. Marinello suggested to the officer that someone else might not agree that the prints were a match. Crowe said that was not the case. Marinello pointed out that the latent print was not as crisp in the photograph as the inked impression was, but Crowe said it was clear enough for the match.

Marinello now argued that it was "not unusual to find

palmprints, fingerprints in the particular house the individual resides in." Crowe acknowledged the point.

Then Marinello listed a number of items on which no identifiable print had been found as if that would lessen the import of Crowe's earlier testimony.

On redirect Cotter asked, "Officer Crowe, you indicated the palmprint of Robert Golub was found on the molding."

"That is correct."

"Can you tell us whether Robert Golub, when he touched that molding with his palm, had the reddish-brown substance on his hand at the time he touched the molding or whether the substance was in the molding and then he touched the molding with his palm?"

"From the shape of the impression the substance was on the palm of the hand and not on the wall."

"Can you tell us how you, as an expert witness, can determine that?"

"Looking at the latent impression and the photos of the latent impression, the fluid is only on the shape of the latent impression and the characteristics of the ridge formations up until the end of the pattern. If the fluid had been on the wall there would be an overlap on the wall past the impression and the impression would have been within that fluid. In this particular case the latent impression is the fluid."

When Crowe stepped down from the witness stand for the last time, Robert Golub was no longer animated. He was as he had been at the beginning of the trial, as he had been throughout his fifteen hours of interrogation the previous year, sitting stoically in his chair, his impassive face revealing nothing, except for the steady, uncontrollable blinking of his eyes.

Seventeen

Dr. Leslie Lukash, the medical examiner who had performed Kelly's autopsy, was called to testify on Monday, March 12. A native of the Bronx and a graduate of Tulane University School of Medicine, he had specialized in pathology and joined the Nassau County Medical Examiner's Office in 1952. He had been Chief Medical Examiner since 1957. He was known for his expressive testimony and his ability to reduce complex medical issues to simple terms that juries could readily comprehend. He was distinguished in appearance with a shock of white hair.

As he spoke a hush descended over the courtroom. Victoria Tinyes had elected not to attend what would surely be graphic testimony, though Linda Player and another of Victoria's sisters were there as was Richard Tinyes.

Since the autopsy the previous year Lukash had analyzed his findings and now meticulously reconstructed in explicit detail the terrible last moments of Kelly's life. Enlarged photographs of the girl's destroyed body were on display, and with a pointer Lukash indicated the areas which supported his conclusions.

It was to be understood, he said, that there had been a fierce struggle. During this Kelly had been punched in the mouth once or twice, then her head had been banged against the floor or perhaps a wall. The force of the blows had been sufficient to move her brain within the skull and to have caused damage. She was beaten savagely about the head and entire tufts of hair were pulled from her scalp. By then unconscious, she was strangled by a pair of human hands. Lukash extended his own hands and demonstrated the act. Her face had become swollen and lividly discolored until it was nearly black.

While Lukash spoke Richard Tinyes turned a bright red and swallowed repeatedly as his eyes moistened. His sisters-in-law were weeping.

The strangulation, Lukash said, had been sufficient alone to have caused death. Kelly's clothes were ripped from her, torn apart in many cases, buttons popping and seams renting apart. The girl had been stomped repeatedly on the neck and chest and was cut many, many times across her torso. There was evidence she had been kicked in the neck and she had a scrape on her chest which had possibly come from the sole of a shoe. Her throat was slashed to the backbone, but the cause of death had been strangulation and multiple injuries to her neck.

There were on Kelly's body two bite marks. One had been inflicted while she was still alive, the other after her death. Her sexual organs were then mutilated.

Lukash went on to explain that this had been a protracted assault. "It took twenty to thirty minutes between impact [the blow to her mouth] and death to occur, in my opinion," he testified.

The jurors recoiled from the graphic photograph and from Lukash's description of the murder. One young man, sitting in the first row of the jury box, winced and grimaced repeatedly, then placed his hand over his mouth. Other jurors could not bear to look at the pictures for more than a few seconds at a time, then had to turn away. Robert stared straight before him.

Lukash said the examination of Kelly's body established the time of death as sometime between noon and six P.M. Since Kelly was known to have entered the Golub house at 3:10 that Friday, the time of death had been from then until six. When Richie Tinyes had pounded on the door and called out for his sister, she was being slaughtered in the basement of the Golubs' house.

The killer had taken a piece of broken glass, gripped it with the folded blue tablecloth, then performed most of the slicing of Kelly's body with it. Under microscopic examination "railroad track" cuts consistent with the edge of glass were apparent along the edges of the wounds. The massive mutilation had been most likely performed with the bayonet.

At the noon recess Victoria Tinyes's sisters pursued the Golubs as they were leaving the courthouse. "How can you live in that house?" one screamed. Court officers closed ranks about the Golubs. So distraught were the pursuing pair that one fainted in the hallway as they were confronting John Golub and his wife. Elizabeth paused and turned at one point as if to respond, but her husband placed his hand on her back and pushed her ahead.

After the lunch break Marinello asked Lukash if there might have been more than one assailant.

"I can't tell you if there was more than one individual or not."

Marinello pressed the point, noting the extensive neck injuries. Could those be "an indication of more than one person?" he asked again.

"Could be."

Cotter raised the point on redirect. Lukash testified that there was "nothing inconsistent" with a single assailant for that matter.

The following day Lowell Levine, the forensic odontologist, was called to testify. For months Wells had waited for the results of his comparison of the two bite marks on Kelly's body with the models of Robert Golub's teeth Levine had prepared. Only on that Monday had the doctor finally shared his conclusions.

Levine had been a dentist since 1963. Over the years he had become specially trained as a forensic odontologist, working in that capacity for more than ten years with the New York City Chief Medical Examiner. After that he had worked with the New York State Police and the Nassau County Medical Examiner's Office. Cotter asked him to explain what it was he did.

"You'll hear the term forensic dentist, forensic odontology. Basically it's that branch of the science of dentistry which deals with the examination, handling, and reporting of dental evidence in the interests of justice. There are basically three areas that the forensic odontologist or dentist works in. One is identification of either burned, fragmented, mutilated, or otherwise unidentifiable human remains. Another area is the examination and documentation of traumatic injuries to the face, teeth, jaws, gums, that type of thing. The third area that we work in is the examination of bite-mark evidence which we find in certain types of cases."

Levine identified the many jurisdictions in which he

had offered expert testimony. He had been one of the odontologists who had identified the remains of infamous Nazi doctor Joseph Mengele in Brazil in 1985 and in 1984 he had helped identify the exhumations from mass graves of thousands of "missing" in Argentina. He had identified a bite mark made by Ted Bundy and was the only odontologist used by the U.S. Army to identify MIAs returned from Vietnam. Cotter asked him to describe what he did.

"We examine the patternage which is what bite marks are, usually in tissue, and sometimes other things, of both living and dead victims which have been left at crime scenes. . . . It is an injury like a bruise in which there is specific patternage left by the object that has left the bruise."

Levine described the human jaw and teeth and how it was possible to determine who had made a bite mark. "The teeth that usually leave some pattern are the four incisors, upper or lower or both, and the two canine or cuspids, the eyeteeth. Next to them sometimes the bicuspids." Certain teeth left a rectangular pattern, others were a triangle, still others left an impression in the form of a diamond.

"Everybody has a set of teeth that are unique to that person and there are a number of things that individualize them. One is shape caused by the wear patterning. Another are things dentists do, such as caps, crowns. You have tipping, turning, because of various positions of the mouth teeth wear differently. You can have missing teeth . . ."

Levine explained the procedure he had followed in this case, comparing the pattern injuries with the photographs and models he had prepared.

"What can you tell us about the pattern injuries that you found in the medical examiner's photographs in this particular case?"

"What I found is that there are two areas that had patternage consistent with human bite marks."

"Were they, in fact, human bite marks?"

"They are human bite marks."

"Have you arrived at an opinion with a reasonable degree of medical certainty with respect to the individual that made those pattern injuries to the victim?"

"Yes, sir, I have."

"And what is your opinion as to the identification of the individual who made those injuries?"

"They were made by Robert Golub."

Levine went on to testify that one of the two bites on Kelly's body, the one on her buttocks, came from Robert's upper teeth. A bite on her neck "could have been caused" by Robert's lower teeth. Levine used the plaster model to demonstrate on his own skin how he reached some of his conclusions. Life-sized photographs of the wounds and a plaster impression of Robert's teeth were passed to the jurors.

Marinello objected that such categorical statements of fact by Levine constituted new evidence of which he had not been aware prior to the trial. Without conceding the point Cotter asked the questions differently.

"Are you, in fact, saying it is him and nobody else?" he asked.

"Yes," Levine replied, saying he was "ninety-nine point nine hundred ninety-nine percent to infinity" certain that the bite mark was Robert Golub's.

"There were no characteristics that would exclude this defendant?"

"That is correct, sir."

The plaster model of Golub's teeth had ended up on the table where he sat with his lawyer. Victoria Tinyes alternately stared at the model in horror then glared at Robert. Finally, she stalked out of the courtroom.

The following day Cotter concluded the People's case against Robert Golub. The prosecutor had called twenty-eight witnesses and consumed five weeks to present his case. But despite what appeared to be a very strong circumstantial case, John Nolan was concerned about its outcome. Just months earlier a murderer's lawyer had convinced a jury that his preppy client had accidentally killed a police sergeant's daughter during "rough sex," despite a taped confession. As a result he had received a greatly reduced sentence.

In the Golub case there was no confession and no eyewitness. Jurors were always uncomfortable convicting someone without one or the other. What they had was circumstantial evidence subject to more than one interpretation. Juries could be persuaded to all kinds of strange propositions by a defense lawyer, and this was just the type of sensational trial in which something like that could occur.

The local TV news channel 12 had covered nearly every hour of the trial and there were households on Long Island which followed the case religiously. As the defense prepared to make its presentation, a television reporter asked John Golub about reports that he was considering obtaining a court order to stop the harassment.

"We just don't have the time to do it," he answered. "Now it's to the point even if we have to take a day off from court we have to find a way to do it."

"Is it possible to get an order of protection without a crime being committed?"

"I don't think an order of protection has to do with a crime. I think it's to do with your civil rights. We have rights, same as they have rights. We're not supposed to be subject to verbal harassment and threats when we walk down the street. I shouldn't even have to listen to them in court, in the hallway here, screaming and hollering at me or my wife and we shouldn't have to put up with that. I think it's illegal, but obviously maybe I'm wrong. They're doing it. I feel if I was here doing it I'd be thrown right out. It's not working that way."

"Does it make you a little nervous coming here?"

"I'm not nervous coming here. Makes us nervous going home, yes. They've already stopped my wife's car. Stopped her from going in the house, you know physically blocked the road. So what if they're going to do that again, you know. We had an incident the other day. I don't think they blocked the road knowing I was coming up the street, but the road was blocked when I got there. I had to go around a car. I got verbal harassment for going around the car."

The primary tactic of Marinello during the presentation of the People's case had been to question every fact, every procedure, and to review the basis for findings to the point of exhaustion. At times the cross-examinations had been excruciating in length and repetition, continuing until members of the jury could be seen nodding off. The question on everyone's mind was whether or not Robert

Golub would take the stand in his own defense, and that was one question Marinello wasn't answering.

On Monday, March 19, 1990, Marinello called John Golub to testify in his son's behalf. He suggested that an intruder could have entered his basement and committed the murder then fled unseen. Some months earlier the side basement door had been damaged and John Golub did not believe he had repaired it as well as he could have.

"If the door was broken which is what I maintain, a hundred people could have had access to the house," he claimed.

Even though he acknowledged signing a consent form, he insisted the police had overstepped themselves in searching his house. As for the door to his son's bedroom, Robert's father testified he had removed it in anger and "threw it away" because his son was constantly borrowing his clothes without permission.

John Golub's desire to help his son's case was apparent, but in the end he did more harm than good. Under cross-examination he was argumentative and demonstrated the same smart-ass manner toward Cotter that John Jay had given to Detective Sharkey. Asked how his side basement door came to be damaged, he admitted that Robert had kicked the door in months earlier to gain access to the house because he had forgotten his front-door key.

Pressed on the point about his reason for removing the door to Robert's bedroom, he acknowledged there had been more to it than his earlier testimony suggested. His wife feared that their son would overload electrical outlets with his fish tank, fan, and appliances. She was also concerned because he often had friends in his bedroom until three A.M. She disapproved and asked for the door to be taken off. What he did not say was that apparently it would not have been enough simply to have asked Robert not to have friends over so late.

Examining a photograph taken of the basement side door the day Kelly was found, John Golub admitted that it did not look disturbed and that any intruder would have had to repair it just as he had, then either crawl out a basement window or sneak up the stairs and exit out the front door.

The bayonet was his, he admitted. It was usually found in one of the smaller rooms in the basement.

And, John Golub testified, the day before the murder Robert had stolen a collection of watches from his father and pawned them for $275. A collection that John Golub had kept a portion of in the attaché cases in the basement.

When Elizabeth Golub was called to the stand, there were gasps from the Tinyes family. Elizabeth was thin by this time, with a gaunt, haunted look. Watching her, week after week, Wells had become concerned she would become ill during the trial. She testified with a quavering voice, waving her hands in front of her, glancing nervously toward the jury periodically.

"With respect to the deceased, Kelly Ann Tinyes," Marinello asked, "did you know her from the neighborhood?"

"Yes."

"Did you ever speak to her in the neighborhood before March of 1989?"

"Oh, yes."

"You had a conversation with her previously?"

"Yes."

"While you were in the house prior to March third,

1989, did you ever receive a phone call from Kelly Ann Tinyes?"

"Not for me, for my son John Jay, yes."

"Well, did you pick up the phone?"

"Yes."

"Did you recognize who was calling?"

"Yes. I asked who called. That's what I used to do when I answered the phone. I always say, 'Who's calling?' "

"When did you receive the telephone call?"

"The exact dates I can't give you, but it's two or three times she called the house."

"Okay. Two or three times over what period of time?"

"I'd say from maybe October 1989."

"When she called did she ask to speak to someone?"

"John Jay."

"And what did you do with respect to these phone calls?"

"I just gave them to John Jay. Many times he got calls from girls."

"In the particular neighborhood have you ever seen Kelly Ann Tinyes speaking to your son, John Jay?"

"Yes, several times."

"Would you indicate those particular times in which you saw them."

"One evening I came home and I pulled down the driveway and she was on the side of my husband's car talking with John Jay up the driveway. That was one incident. Another time it was like a three-way conversation between her and the girl next door and John Jay up on my driveway. I believe it was the week preceding this that I had come home. I remember it was a nice evening. Mrs. Stonel was outside. I parked my car in the street and the neighborhood boys were playing football down at the end toward Peninsula Boulevard. I looked up . . . and John Jay was talking with Kelly. . . ."

"Any other occasions did you see them speaking together?"

"Yes. Sometimes Kelly used to play in front of Nichol's house or between the homes, tennis with the rackets and occasionally John Jay and Michael and them would all engage in a conversation. They were not total strangers. These kids were brought up together."

Elizabeth Golub identified a girlfriend of Robert's who had been in her son's bedroom in the days before the murder. She had shoulder-length, brown hair and this might have been the source of the nine-inch strand of hair found there by police.

During her testimony the Tinyes family exchanged perplexed looks. To their knowledge, Kelly did not know John Jay Golub and had certainly never been in the Golubs' driveway.

Elizabeth's entire demeanor changed when Cotter rose to ask her questions. She suddenly became very aggressive and short-tempered.

"Mrs. Golub," Cotter began, "when you went home on Friday afternoon, Paul Zerella wasn't at the house, was he?"

"I didn't see him, no."

"And Paul Zerella picked your son up Saturday at noon?"

"I don't know what time he picked him up."

"Well, did he come in his van and pick—"

"I don't know," Elizabeth interrupted. "I was busy with the police officers, McVetty and the other one. I was in a state of confusion. I was trying to get the story together."

Judge Goodman asked, "Did you see him come in his van, that's—"

Interrupting again, Elizabeth said, "No! He asked me that."

Judge Goodman sat back in his chair. "Next question."

And so it went.

For a year now Wells had dreaded Nawrocki's testimony. He had told Wells that the latent print located by the body was not Robert Golub's. Based on that Wells had put the information in the affidavit. Then Crowe had made his match. Now Marinello called Nawrocki to testify on behalf of Robert Golub.

The defense attorney dwelled on the detective's years of experience and expert training in identifying fingerprints. Then Nawrocki testified that he had been the first one to examine the molding taken from the Golubs' basement. The molding had been preserved in a wooden box with a glass top and was handed to him. He testified to the detailed process and examination he had performed and that he had been unable to find any skin frictions that were identifiable. His conclusion had been that there were no latent prints on the molding that were valuable for identification purposes.

Nawrocki then gave the molding and photographs to Off. Ron Crowe to complete, claiming that he had not as yet formed a final opinion. Crowe had come to him with specific reference points and Nawrocki had checked the latent against Robert Golub's inked print.

"The latent impression was identified as the left palm-print of Robert Golub," he testified.

The latent print had been subsequently analyzed by the FBI and confirmed their opinion. It was Robert Golub's print on the molding.

Marinello called Wells to testify on behalf of the defendant. Wells took the stand with his poker face and testified that he had twenty-four years' experience as a police officer. He was the lead detective on the Kelly Ann Tinyes investigation. Asked about the affidavit he had filed with the court in which he stated the latent print did not belong to Robert Golub, Wells replied that the information in the affidavit had been based upon his "information and belief" at that stage of the investigation. He never claimed it was definitive.

"Did you make this statement, Detective Wells, with respect to the affidavit?" Marinello asked to drive his point home for the jury. " 'The police department has received latent and palm impressions from Robert Golub, Chris Earle, and Mick Donnell. Members of the Scientific Investigations Bureau have eliminated these three individuals as the possible source of the bloody latent print.' Did you make that statement?"

"Yes, sir."

Marinello said, "I have no other questions."

Eighteen

Now Marinello called defense experts to rebuke the People's presentation. This was a case built entirely of circumstantial evidence and the jury's faith in those experts Cotter had called would be a major factor in deliberations. In cases such as this it was imperative that the defense respond with its own distinguished experts and by their testimony either refute outright the opinions offered by the People's experts, or muddy the waters. Nothing, Marinello would suggest, is ever black-and-white.

In recent years a veritable cottage industry has developed to provide defense expert witnesses. There are doctors and scientists who have given up private practices to testify in court, charging from $150 to $500 an hour for their services. To find such witnesses all a defense attorney has to do is turn to the back pages of *Trial Magazine* and peruse the advertisements.

Technical Advisory Service of Philadelphia is a leading company in providing such experts. It lists fifteen thousand of them in forty-four hundred areas of specialty and in thirty years of business has referred 133,000 clients. "I always say that you can look at any case that makes news and the attorney will come into our office the next day, and that's what usually happens," the director commented at the time of the Golub murder trial.

Marinello had done his homework. The first expert to testify on behalf of Robert Golub was Jeffrey Burkes, Chief Forensic consultant on odontology for the New York City Medical Examiner's Office. He explained that human skin "was never designed to be a medium for picking up dental impressions."

Based on his examination of the same evidence Dr. Levine had used to make his determination, Burkes concluded that the buttock bite mark on Kelly had not been made by Robert Golub. A rotated cuspid on Robert's lower jaw did not appear to have left any matching impression on the wound and there were "other marks" that were "inconsistent" with his teeth. "It is not a match . . . This pattern does not appear to be made by these teeth."

Burkes went on to testify that he was not even certain the mark on Kelly's neck was from a human bite. "I have serious doubts that it was a bite mark. I cannot say that it is."

On cross-examination Burkes testified that he spent comparatively little time, perhaps fifteen percent, on forensic medicine and only a fraction of that fraction on bite-mark identification.

Manhattan serologist Lawrence Kobilinsky testified next as to the DNA tests performed by Lifecodes. Lorah McNally was a former student of his for two years and he had sponsored her for her master's degree.

Kobilinsky said it had been inappropriate for McNally to mix the A samples taken from the top of two of the attaché cases. Asked about the dangers of mixing blood then performing the more generalized genetic marker tests Birdsall had performed, Kobilinsky detailed how erroneous readings could result. But later he acknowledged that it was accepted procedure to mix stains in order to obtain enough blood on which to perform DNA tests, just so the results were properly interpreted.

Throughout Kobilinsky's long testimony Cotter frequently sparred with the witness. At points the testimony became so detailed and convoluted in its description of the various blood tests, it appeared to tax the concentration of the jurors.

At one point Marinello asked Kobilinsky if Robert's blood could have been "spilled" on the tablecloth by someone other than Golub? Kobilinsky answered "Yes." Under cross-examination Cotter demanded to know if the serologist had any proof that evidence tampering had occurred. "Are you saying that police officer Birdsall took blood and put it on the samples?"

"That's possible."

If that was the case then Birdsall could have put blood "on all" the exhibits he had tested.

"Yes."

Did Kobilinsky have any evidence to support a claim of evidence tampering?

"None that I could tell," the witness admitted.

Asked about his review of Birdsall's procedures, he testified they had "to a large degree" been proper.

On Monday, March 26, Marinello began the seventh week of trial by calling Dr. Norman Sperber, Chief Forensic Dentist for San Diego [California] County, to the stand. Sperber was world renowned in the field of forensic odontology for having established national identification standards for bite-mark analysis. There were those who claimed that while Dr. Lowell Levine had seized the limelight and built his reputation with high-profile cases, it was Sperber who was the foremost forensic odontologist.

Sperber testified that he had examined the same photographs and models as Levine, then he had performed independent tests himself by using the model of Robert's teeth to "bite" into Styrofoam as well as the arm of a volunteer. He had then photographed the results.

As he explained his analysis of the results, one of the jurors bit into one of his own hands several times, then examined the impressions closely. The other jurors hung on Sperber's every word.

Sperber testified in a very excited manner that appeared to be his usual style that it "would be impossible for those models to cause the marks on the neck." He was not certain the mark had been made by a human bite, but if it had, it would have been inflicted by someone with a missing upper front tooth, a tooth Robert Golub had intact.

Asked by Marinello about the bite on Kelly's buttock, Sperber answered, "Those models I was presented with could not possibly have caused those marks . . ."

He explained that Robert Golub's dental cast showed that both of his lower canine teeth were rotated, a "most unusual" condition, and that there was no evidence of that rotation in the photographs of the bite mark on the buttock.

Cotter pressed Sperber during a vigorous cross-examination and the doctor acknowledged that the arc of Robert's four front teeth matched the buttock bite, but beyond that made no concessions. "It was so obvious," Sperber said, "that those teeth could not have caused those marks just by those rotated teeth."

The more Cotter pressed, the more agitated Sperber behaved. At one point Cotter admonished the defense witness, "Doctor, relax. You don't have to get excited."

"I'm very . . ."

"Gentlemen," Judge Goodman said, "please, please."

"He's shaking his head and dancing in his seat," Cotter explained.

Marinello objected. "Judge, I ask the court to admonish the district attorney."

"Please, Mr. Cotter," Judge Goodman said, "ask questions. No comments."

Sperber wanted his chance as well. "I think you ought to relax a little bit, Mr. Cotter."

Still another serologist testified concerning DNA testing. He was Dr. Simon Ford, a doctor of biochemistry from the University of Bristol [England]. He had been a molecular biologist since 1977 and had worked in genetic research in New York City and Los Angeles for four years. In 1986 he became involved in forensic DNA analysis. He had reviewed three reports by Lifecodes in this case as well as the charts themselves.

"Can you make a match with respect to a particular sample based on visualization or determining where the bands lined up alone without any other criteria?" Marinello asked.

"No."

Marinello concluded with, "Dr. Ford, based upon what your analysis has been in this case and looking at the particular [charts] and reports that were generated by Lifecodes in this particular case, can you indicate with a reasonable degree of scientific certainty whether or not you could declare a match with respect to the blood samples of the defendant in this particular case?"

"Not to a reasonable degree of scientific certainty, no."

During cross-examination Cotter pressed Ford. If he could not testify the blood samples matched anyone perhaps he had found they excluded certain persons. "Using the [charts] can you exclude individuals from being the contributor of the DNA on those attaché cases?"

"Yes, it is possible to exclude individuals."

"Did you exclude anyone as being the source using these [charts]?"

There was a long pause.

"Yes or no," Cotter asked, to coax an answer.

There was another long pause. "To what degree of certainty?" Ford wanted to know.

"When somebody's excluded, they're excluded for good, are they not?"

"Yes, sir, but with respect can I point out the dilemma that I'm in . . ."

"No. Answer my questions if you can, yes or no. When a person is excluded, when you find a band that definitely does not match, that person is excluded as being the individual who left the DNA."

"No."

"Do you mean if you find a band that doesn't match up you could still possibly match that individual?"

"Correct." Ford explained there could be a typing error, something that gave a high number of very high false negatives when two DNA prints were traced.

Next Marinello called Peter DeForest, professor of Criminalistics at John Jay College of Criminal Justice at the City University of New York, and an expert on hair analysis. DeForest had reviewed Schiraldi's findings, then compared the nine-inch strand of hair taken from Robert's bed with a strand taken from the girl who had been in his room that week and one from Kelly.

DeForest testified that hair evaluation was a very involved and complex process which is highly subjective. In his opinion the girlfriend's hair was "distinctly different" from Kelly's. It had been dyed or bleached unlike either Kelly's or the hair found in Robert's bedding. Comparing Kelly's directly with the one from Robert's bed, he had also been "unable to conclude that the hair came from the same source," though he stated, "I was also unable to eliminate that possibility." In addition, he was unable to rule out the possibility that the hair from Robert's bedding had not come from his girlfriend.

The testimony of expert witnesses for the defense had continued through the week amid mounting speculation as to whether Robert Golub would take the stand in his own defense. He was the one person in the courtroom who had to respond, and he was the only person the court could not order to speak.

Placing an accused felon on the witness stand is always a risky enterprise in any criminal trial. Even falsely accused persons can behave on the stand in a guilty manner, especially if the crime committed was especially heinous. The pressure in such a situation can be overpowering. Innocent persons are also not necessarily honest ones and not above lying on key points if it casts them in a better light. Being caught in even a single, relatively harmless lie would impeach every truthful denial made under oath.

There were other risks as well. A skilled cross-examination can potentially make even the most innocent defendant appear guilty. Further, if the accused had a criminal record it could be brought to the attention of the jury and possibly prejudice it against the defendant. After all, if he had committed one crime why not another?

In the case of accused murderers the general legal opinion is that placing the defendant on the stand is tantamount to malpractice. So it came as no surprise to the legal community when, with the conclusion of DeForest's testimony, Marinello rested the defense case having not called Robert to testify.

Cotter had an opportunity to rebuke portions of the defense's case with additional witnesses so he called still another odontologist. His testimony was sprinkled with phrases such as "matched exactly" and "measured exactly." As for Robert's teeth and the mark found on Kelly's buttock, "My opinion is they definitely did cause that mark."

At the conclusion of seven weeks of testimony, Judge Goodman addressed the jurors.

"Ladies and gentlemen of the jury, the case is now completed. You will no longer hear any witnesses or see any more exhibits. All that remains in this trial is the final summations by both attorneys. Summation will start Monday morning. Defense counsel will sum up first. The district attorney will then sum up, and then I will charge you and you will retire to deliberate."

The jurors were instructed to bring a change of clothing as they would be sequestered during the deliberative process. The trial was placed in recess until Monday.

Clutching her well-worn prayer book, Elizabeth

Golub left the courtroom. Over that weekend she went grocery shopping. For months now it had not been possible for her to appear publicly without running the risk of someone recognizing her. These were often unpleasant encounters. Outside the store a casual acquaintance approached her. Elizabeth had no answers about what was going on. "It's in God's hands now. I don't think he did it; I just can't believe he did it. I just hope there is justice. Justice for Kelly and for Robert."

Marinello had motioned the court the last day of testimony to allow the jury to consider a reduced charge of first degree manslaughter. On Monday, April 2, Judge Goodman ruled that the death of Kelly Ann Tinyes was unquestionably an intentional act, therefore not manslaughter, and denied the motion.

But before the jury entered the courtroom and final summations could commence, Marinello had another motion. This time he wanted a mistrial, claiming that the intense media coverage of the trial had prejudiced the jury. Judge Goodman was clearly perturbed that such a motion had not been made the previous Thursday at the conclusion of testimony so he would have the long weekend to consider his decision. Marinello explained that he had not made the motion at that time because there was going to be still more media coverage over the weekend.

Judge took a brief recess then returned to the bench. Reading from a prepared decision, he said there was ". . . nothing to demonstrate that this jury has not followed the court's admonitions. The court finds no factual basis to poll this jury on the issue of publicity. The motion is denied. Get the jury in."

It was not Wells's custom to attend closing argument in any of his trials. He thought it demonstrated an unusual and possibly biased interest on his part. But no case he had ever worked before in his long career had moved him as this one had. He had nearly died trying to catch Robert Golub and so, for the only time in any case, he sat with the spectators and listened to what the lawyers had to say.

Marinello spoke for over two hours. He began quietly, with his hands placed behind his back as he paced slowly before the jury. As the intensity of his argument rose, so too did the volume of his voice. He frowned frequently and spoke with fierce intensity.

"In this case the defense has had to overcome untold facts," he said after thanking the jurors for their attentiveness. "Things that don't come across on the witness stand. The atmosphere that permeates this courtroom. Untold factors. The sympathetic nature of what happened to this young girl. The sympathy for the family of the deceased. Those are things that you can't quantify in this courtroom, because the courtroom is a very sterile and artificial atmosphere. The defense has to overcome . . . to chip away and bang away at every piece of evidence . . .

"You know that the entire case rests on circumstantial evidence. There is no direct evidence linking the defendant to the commission of this crime. . . . There's no doubt that the deceased Kelly Ann Tinyes entered the Golub home that day. There's no doubt that her body was found in the basement closet. That's not the issue."

Marinello explained that Cotter had attempted to systematically eliminate the other persons present in the Golub house that day, leaving the jury with just the defendant. "Who else could have murdered Kelly Ann Tinyes? But when you consider that question, you have to consider other factors and other evidence in this case. . . . Have the People proved the defendant's guilt beyond a reasonable doubt? That's why we're here in this courtroom. Not what you might think the defendant did, not whether or not the defendant had an opportunity to commit this crime, but have the People proved it here? . . . The answer to that question is, they have not.

"The lack of evidence in this case is just as important and maybe more important than the evidence the district attorney produced here. . . . I suggest to you what they don't have is equally important and creates a reasonable doubt. . . . You know there are reasonable doubts in this case and you only need one reasonable doubt to acquit . . . I can sit here from now until the end of the day and point them out to you, one after another, reasonable doubt after reasonable doubt. The mystery of Eighty-one Horton Road in this case certainly is a mystery. There were more unanswered questions at the end of this case than there were at the beginning . . ."

Casting doubt wherever he could, clouding issues, diverting the jurors' attention from the single line of logic they must follow in the People's case to convict his client, Marinello attacked Cotter's case, point by point. Robert Golub sat in his place in a gray suit with a plum tie and a fresh haircut, looking every bit the preppy Marinello wanted to present him as. How could this young man murder anyone? he suggested with every nod of his head toward his client.

"As the defendant sits there now he's got the presumption of innocence. He's no different than any other human being that has been tried in a criminal case. He's

no ogre as a result of the test that's been produced
here . . .

"The easiest thing in the world would be to come
back with a verdict of guilty in this case. It's another
matter to truly try the evidence in this case." Raising
his voice he shouted, "To truly try it and not be intimidated by a verdict of guilty here! If somebody yells at
you during the course of these summations, or the district attorney shows the photographs of the deceased,
the horror of this crime, it is very easy to be intimidated." Lowering his voice he intoned, "Don't let your-
selves be intimidated into a verdict of guilty."

The police arrested no one during the first weeks, he
said, because they had no evidence. When they did arrest Robert Golub finally "they had a partial palmprint
which they say was made in blood . . . They arrested
the defendant and they set upon, after that date, not to
gather evidence in this case, but to prove his guilt. Not
to assemble evidence to prove his guilt, but to *fashion*
the evidence to prove his guilt, to *create* the evidence
to prove his guilt in this case . . .

"How do we know about the partial palmprint in this
case? . . . We know, and this has only been shown by
the defense who called these witnesses, the defense had
to call Detective Wells, who sat here for nine weeks
and was not called by the prosecution. The carrying detective in this case, we had to call him to say during
the course of these proceedings he signed an affidavit
under oath to the court . . . that Robert Golub was
eliminated as being one who left the print on this molding. Not that they couldn't identify the print, not that
they had difficulty finding a reference point in the
palmprint as the detectives testified to, but they elimi-

nated him! And that's what they arrested the defendant on. An eliminated palmprint! This is not Robert Golub's palmprint but we are going to arrest him anyway . . .

"Then what happens after that? Police officer Crowe . . . pulls out a lottery ticket and says magically, 'I identified a partial palmprint of the defendant.' What does the defense do, with respect to that testimony? The defense calls police officer Crowe's supervisor, Detective Sergeant Nawrocki." Crowe's supervisor couldn't make an identification, and if the defense hadn't called these two witnesses, would the jury have known about it? The implication was, no, the jury would not have known.

"They create this evidence . . . Does the evidence hold up here? Is it really there or has it been created by the prosecution? . . . The evidence wasn't there to begin with in March of 1989 and it's not here in this courtroom over a year later, and nothing you can do and nothing that you can fashion will change that. . . ."

Cotter had established no motive, Marinello insisted, had not proven whether it was sexual or psychotic behavior. He questioned the conduct of the police, arguing misconduct because Birdsall had tested twenty-two bloodstains on the blue tablecloth before finding Robert's blood at the twenty-third spot. "Am I suggesting that the police officer placed the blood of this defendant on the cloth?" he intoned. "You must make that determination."

Marinello told the jurors that if they weighed each side's expert witnesses and don't know who to believe, "Isn't that reasonable doubt?"

Marinello then threw the names of the investigating officers out one by one with an angry sneer to denigrate their reputations. "Birdsall." "McVetty." "Nolan." "Wells." He paused after each to let his contempt for their conduct sink in.

He then attacked the forensic evidence, arguing in effect that because the naked eye cannot see the distinctions in blood that McNally had testified to they did not exist, much like a man arguing that because you cannot see air there is no such thing. "How can you measure what you can't see?" The jury appeared to hang on his every word.

He concluded by reminding the jurors that they would not hear from him again. "Do me this favor, when Mr. Cotter makes his closing arguments, ask yourself, 'How would Mr. Marinello have addressed that particular issue, what would he have said about that?' " He asked for a verdict of "not guilty" and concluded with, "Each and every one of you has to look into your souls." Having made a dramatic, powerful presentation, he sat down beside Robert.

Cotter spoke to the jury last as the People bore the burden of proof. He began by re-creating the events of the last day of peace on Horton Road. He described what was done to Kelly, then asked the jury to consider this. Who hit her? Who ripped her clothes from her? Who mutilated her? Who stuffed her into a sleeping bag?

In the chair Wells had occupied during the trial, Cotter displayed a large photograph of Kelly, the last school picture taken of her. Let's not forget why we are here, he said. Kelly Ann Tinyes is the focus of this trial, not Robert Golub. He referred often to the picture as he spoke, calling the jurors' attention to it repeatedly.

There are, he told the jury, only four suspects: John

Jay, Donnell, Earle, and Robert Golub. And there was not one shred of evidence to indicate anyone other than the defendant was anywhere near the crime scene in the basement.

Step by step he recounted the People's case. Robert's bloody palmprint was found by the body. The serology tests alone narrowed the search for the killer to Robert, the DNA results were an even more powerful statement that he had been there. Then there was the hair strand and finally the two bite marks. The experts had testified how they had come to their conclusions. Their reports had been available, the procedures followed known. The defense expert witnesses had prepared no reports, not been subject to the same rigorous scrutiny the People's witnesses had survived.

The jury had been spellbound by Marinello's more artful presentation, less attentive to Cotter's.

Cotter reminded the jury that Marinello had claimed there were one hundred reasonable doubts, but never pointed out a single one. He held up again the photograph of lovely Kelly, who was smiling in her youth and innocence. "Kelly Ann Tinyes, March 3, 1989, before Robert Golub." Then he held up a picture of her horribly mutilated body. "And Kelly Ann Tinyes, March 3, 1989, after Robert Golub . . .

"Can you imagine doing this to someone?" He paused. "No, you cannot. Because we are not like him."

Nineteen

Judge Goodman delivered his final instructions to the jury that same Monday. In order to find Robert Golub guilty of murder the People were required to prove beyond a reasonable doubt three elements. First, that on or about the third day of March 1989, the defendant caused the death of Kelly Ann Tinyes. Second, the defendant intended to cause her death. "It is not necessary," Judge Goodman said, "for the People to establish that the intent to kill was present in the mind of the defendant for any period of time before he caused the death of Kelly Ann Tinyes. It is sufficient if you find that such intent to kill was in the mind of the defendant when he caused her death." Third, the defendant's acts caused the death.

"If you find all three of these elements then you may find the defendant guilty of the crime of murder in the second degree. On the other hand, if you find that the People have failed to prove to your satisfaction beyond a reasonable doubt any one or more of these three elements then you must find the defendant not guilty of murder in the second degree."

Judge Goodman dismissed the four alternate jurors and late that afternoon the jury filed from the courtroom to begin deliberations. There was a single moment of excitement when a spectator, his face filled with hate, leaned forward in his seat and bared his teeth at the parents of Robert Golub. It was Tuesday, April 3, 1990, thirteen months since the murder of Kelly Ann Tinyes.

For the rest of that day the jurors reviewed the evidence. They spent the night in a nearby hotel, sequestered from media coverage while they considered their decision. Wednesday morning they resumed deliberations.

There is no way to know how long a jury will consider a case. There is no way to know if a quick verdict is good or bad, or for that matter if a slow one is any better. Wells hung out at the office, knowing from experience that the call the jury was back could come at any moment, or not for days. He was drained, as empty as he could ever remember being. He was sure there would be a conviction, there *had* to be a conviction. The alternative was unthinkable. But juries were funny creatures. It was never possible to predict what one would do.

Marinello was satisfied that he had rebutted every key point of the People's case. He believed he had demonstrated that experts did disagree as to the results of the testing. It was important that the jury consider not just Cotter's experts, but that they take into account what his had to say as well. He had seen acquittals in murder trials with more evidence for conviction than Cotter had presented in this one.

Back at the Mineola courthouse the jurors were reviewing the evidence. One juror took the plaster model of Robert's teeth, pressed it hard against his forearm, then displayed the brief indentations to his fellow jurors as they compared them to the photograph of the bite on Kelly's buttocks. With a ruler they measured the matching points. "The spaces, the distances, and the positioning of the teeth were all exactly alike," one later said, "and for me, that sealed it. We could see it for ourselves."

The jury requested that portions of the trial testimony relating to who had been in the Golubs' house the day of the murder, when they arrived and when they were witnessed departing, be read back to them. This was a highly intelligent jury and the experience of the past two months had brought them closely together. Still the debate in the jury room was vigorous, angry more than once, and emotionally charged.

There was some concern over motive but they found it to be baffling and decided not to dwell on it. "The lack of a motive didn't change the facts or the evidence," one explained.

As the discussion unfolded a consensus developed that the defense expert witnesses had not been as forthcoming in their answers to Cotter's direct questions. They "avoided" the questions as one put it. The defense experts also came across as "mercenaries." One juror said, "I thought they were hired guns."

The jurors discussed possible alternatives to Robert's guilt, then considered the cumulative effect of the evidence. Only after they had organized the evidence officially did they take their first vote. Altogether they deliberated for eight hours before informing the clerk that they were ready to announce a verdict.

One juror had kept some of her opinions to herself for the time being. She had watched Robert Golub closely during the long trial. "He never changed his expression at all," she said much later. "Never during that trial. In the back of your head, it registered that he showed no remorse, no emotion. It was kind of strange."

Wells received word the verdict was about to be announced and met Cotter at the courtroom where they each sat at the usual table. As the nervous jurors filed into the hushed courtroom, Wells noticed that they avoided meeting Robert's eyes. Robert Golub was in the midst of pouring himself a glass of water when a court officer stepped forward and removed the pitcher. Six other officers assumed places between Robert and the spectators. Judge Goodman called the courtroom to order then asked, "Mr. Foreman, has the jury agreed on a verdict?"

The foreman rose. "Yes, we have."

"What is your verdict?"

"Guilty."

Pandemonium erupted as spectators screamed, rising to their feet almost as one. Friends and relatives of the Tinyes family shouted "Yeah!," then loudly "Thank you!" Victoria Tinyes pounded her fists on the railing in front of her and shouted "Yes!"

One Tinyes family member glared at the Golubs and screamed, "Are you happy now? Are you happy?" over and over in such a hostile way that officers physically ejected her in the midst of the chaos as she continued screaming.

Kelly's grandfather shouted at the Golubs also. Robert's sister shot to her feet and screamed back, "I didn't do it!" as her mother began crying.

Not the slightest measure of emotion crossed Robert's face upon hearing the verdict. He looked first at the jury, then to the judge as if hoping somehow he would reverse the decision, then slowly back to the jury. Now he looked at his parents momentarily with an expression that could not be deciphered, the mask of his pleasing, childlike features concealing once again whatever he felt inside.

Court officers found it impossible to restore order and the judge pounded his gavel repeatedly, threatening to have the room cleared if the spectators did not stop. The jurors were stunned and court officials had never before witnessed such a reaction to a verdict. Finally, Judge Goodman gave the order to clear the courtroom so he could proceed with the polling of the jury to be certain the foreman had spoken for all of them.

"Is this your verdict?" the first was asked as the room was being cleared. "Yes." Then the second answered "Yes," then on to each of them until all twelve had spoken their agreement.

Robert rose without prompting and placed his hands behind his back to be handcuffed. John Golub turned so red in the face one court officer thought he was having a heart attack and escorted him into the judge's chamber for observation. Elizabeth Golub laid her head on the rail in front of her and sobbed uncontrollably. After a few moments she was nearly carried from the courtroom to join her husband in the chamber.

The focus of hate had been so altered by the past year's events that not a single insult was hurled at Robert Golub. All of the pejoratives were directed at the members of the Golub family.

Richard Tinyes reacted with anger to the verdict as if he suddenly realized that finding Robert guilty would not return his daughter to life. He stormed from the room, kicking a courthouse display board in the lobby.

Judge Goodman dismissed the jury, then took the customary defense motions made at such a time. Prior to adjournment he ordered that Robert Golub receive a mandatory psychiatric examination prior to sentencing which was set for June 1.

Roberta Grosse was at work when the verdict came in. She learned of it when her boss asked if she wanted to go home for the rest of the day. "Why?" she asked. "They just announced the verdict was guilty, and if you don't want to work the rest of the day I'll understand why."

Roberta thought about the guilty verdict a moment and wondered why she didn't feel better. "All through the trial you think to yourself, finally as soon as the verdict I'll feel so much better, and you think you'll feel relieved. But you don't feel anything . . . Now he's going to appeal . . . he's just going to keep appealing . . . It is a cold, empty feeling."

Later that day, she asked her father about it. "Nothing good will ever come out of this," he told her.

When John Golub was sufficiently recovered he emerged into the hallway where reporters were working the frenzied crowd for reactions. He bore the stony expression he had publicly carried since Kelly's body had been discovered in his basement closet.

The increasingly aggressive Victoria Tinyes spotted her neighbor and told the reporters, "If [Robert] were innocent there would be tears. There would be some emotion. But instead there's nothing. I hope you people record that."

Richard Tinyes drove from the courthouse in his work truck. Mounted on it was a sign that read, "Forever young—Kel."

John Nolan learned of the verdict when another detective burst into his office. "Guilty! They found Golub guilty!" Nolan shot out of his chair and shouted "Yeah!" For months he had avoided letting his detectives know the extent to which he thought their reputation, his own and that of the department, rested on the trial's outcome. Now that weight was lifted from him. They had been vindicated.

Sitting in the courtroom, Wells thought to himself that he had never seen anything like this previously. He had been particularly taken by the sight of the court officer removing the pitcher of water from Robert's hands in the moment before the verdict was announced. He realized it had been a security concern, taking a potential weapon from the prisoner, but at the moment he witnessed the scene it had struck him very differently. The mafia plants a kiss on the lips of the man they are about to kill. Wells had taken the gesture of removing the pitcher as such a sign.

In the hallway Kelly's grandfather told reporters, "I don't want to talk to [the Golubs]. They're dirt to me."

Cotter made brief remarks at the courthouse, then left for his office where fellow prosecutors congratulated him and pumped his hand enthusiastically. Winning a case this big turns any attorney into a momentary superstar. An hour after the verdict Cotter met with reporters in his boss's office and announced with a smile that he was heading for Club Med. "I felt when I walked out of the court I wasn't able to talk to anybody. It may not have been visible, but I literally was shak-

ing. . . . It was the most difficult case I've handled."
Cotter acknowledged there had been some rough moments during the trial. "Sal did a terrific job."

Cotter praised the jury for its hard work. But most of all, after all the restless nights and second-guessing as to how to proceed, he was pleased with his own performance. "We anticipated every avenue [the defense] could have tried to escape through. We slammed every door. They had nowhere to go—trapped!"

Marinello, in contrast, left the courthouse immediately after the verdict, escorted by court officers for his protection, and declined to speak to reporters. He feared this was the moment some crazy might choose to act. He did comment on the outcome later, expressing his surprise at the guilty verdict and his belief that the atmosphere in which the trial had taken place must surely have influenced the decision. "I don't know how any jury could have reached a conclusion in this case without being influenced by things other than the evidence."

On Horton Road it had been raining throughout the day. In anticipation of the verdict Horton Road had been placed under a heavy police presence. As the moment of the decision arrived there were nearly as many reporters as ubiquitous television cameras. As soon as the verdict was announced on television, neighbors spilled from their houses into the rain shouting, "He's guilty! He's guilty!" Reporters roamed through the crowd that had gathered, taking statements, snapping photograph, filming interviews.

A banner was displayed across an overpass on the nearby highway that read, "Death to Golub."

On Horton Road dozens of neighbors and friends

gathered outside the Tinyeses' home in the cold drizzle—they were carrying balloons, flowers, and bottles of champagne; they were hugging and kissing each other. Still more police cars arrived to be certain there was peace on the street. But the Tinyes family elected to stay with relatives and did not come home that night.

Elsewhere the Tinyeses and Players visited with reporters in an atmosphere of relief punctuated with anger. Clutching photographs of her daughter to her, Victoria said, "She's still with us. I was hoping Kelly would walk through the door [at court]. I just want Kelly back."

"There will always be a hundred unanswered questions," Robert Player said. "Why did Kelly go down there? It wasn't like Kelly. It wasn't normal."

One of Victoria's sisters uttered words that spoke for all of them. "Justice was done, but it doesn't bring Kelly back. Kelly's never going to come home."

Richard Tinyes was planning to return to his recently expanded business the next day and attempt to return his life to normalcy. "We may have been cheering in court, but we are crying in our hearts."

The Golubs' house remained dark and no one gathered outside but the media. Late that night the Golubs arrived and were at once besieged by waiting reporters. Asked to comment on the Tinyeses' behavior in court, John said, "We've come to expect that from them." He said he now intended to remain in the neighborhood since it was financially impossible for the family to move.

Earlier that night a neighbor was asked if the verdict

had changed attitudes toward the Golubs. "They're not welcome here," she said, shaking her head. "How could anyone go back and live in that house? I don't think it will ever be over."

She was right. The next day John Golub stood in his yard while Richard Tinyes stood in his and the pair delivered dueling press conferences.

"They have never shown any remorse whatsoever," Richard said of the Golubs.

John Golub was telling reporters of his son's reaction to the verdict. "He was really amazed that he was convicted and that it happened so fast. I thought we were going to have a hung jury. He was convinced if he could get on the stand he could convince the jury that he was innocent."

As for the Tinyes family, "In the beginning we cried as much for their daughter as they did, but they burned it out of us." As for his son, "They're not going to convince me of Robert's guilt until my son tells me himself."

While the trial had suggested that this was a troubled home, in rendering a verdict of guilt it gave no answers to the broader questions. "In what currency did the parents of a killer pay for his crime?" *Newsday* asked in an editorial that weekend. It had proven easier for the Golubs to believe someone broke into their house, lured a neighbor's child into their basement, killed her, and escaped through a window without a trace rather than to accept that their son committed this crime.

In covering the verdict the tabloids milked the subject for every drop of pathos. By taking this approach they had turned a tragedy into a drama in which the two families and their supporters had become players. It was not possible to assess how much the papers' coverage and the television cameras had affected reactions and influenced events, but clearly they had.

The Friday following the verdict John J. O'Grady, the Golub family attorney, delivered a letter to the Nassau County police commissioner. "The principal object of this letter is to put the county of Nassau on notice that an extremely volatile and dangerous condition exists which places the lives of the Golub family and others at risk." The letter contained a long list of allegations of harassment to which the Golubs had been subjected, including verbal abuse, broken windows, paint splattered on cars, and many others. "I find it incredible that not one arrest has resulted from these violent acts, which have continued over a twelve-month period, frequently in plain view of members of the Nassau County Police Department and other peace officers."

Commenting on the letter, John Golub blamed the Tinyes family and his neighbors. He expressed fear that something worse might happen on Horton Road as publicity died down and a police squad car permanently parked on the street was removed. He said he wanted more police protection "before someone gets hurt. Right now there is a lot of media all the time. You want this thing to die off, but it doesn't seem to. I'd like to see it end, but it doesn't seem likely.

"I don't hate Tinyes," he added. "I hate his actions. I hate what he's doing to us. I know he's suffered the loss of his child, but it doesn't excuse what he's doing to us."

Richard Tinyes reacted by saying the Golubs had tried

this approach in the past because they wanted to distract attention from the fact that their son was charged with murdering his daughter. "He's trying to portray himself as the victim, and we're the victims, not him. His son was convicted of brutally killing my daughter. Twelve of Robert's peers convicted him of murder the other day. That's the issue."

The following week John Golub appeared nationally on *Inside Edition,* complaining of neighborhood harassment and asserting an intruder had murdered Kelly. On April 19 Richard Tinyes went on *Geraldo* and fired back, reporting that John Golub had "actually come out on his front lawn with other neighbors present and told me that I killed Kelly and put her in his basement."

John denied it. "I never said that to him. I heard the rumor, all right. But I never shared it with anyone."

Richard made it clear in part just why he was so upset with John Golub. After recounting the mutilation of his daughter, he said, "I think I would have shot my son and shot myself. I don't think I could live with myself knowing that one of my family members did this to a poor little girl in the neighborhood."

In late May a shouting match erupted between John Golub and Richard Tinyes on Horton Road. John later claimed that Richard accused him of participation in Kelly's murder and then shouted, "John Jay is going to be next!" John responded angrily, "You're going to be next!" Then he cursed Richard and a neighbor who was standing nearby.

* * *

On June 1 Robert Golub, wearing a tie and gray

tweed jacket, was taken to court for sentencing. In an extraordinary gesture, eleven of the twelve jurors and four alternates had asked to attend and been given a special place in the courtroom where they were carefully guarded by security officers. The court had received more than one thousand letters bearing more than four thousand signatures urging that life in prison be imposed. Judge Goodman had taken the time to read every one.

For weeks Robert had been angry at the decision that he not testify in his own defense. He told his father repeatedly, "I knew I should have went [sic] on the stand."

Judge Goodman addressed the courtroom. "Ladies and gentlemen. This is a court of law and it demands respect. . . . For today's proceedings I wish to advise all spectators that the court will not tolerate any outburst or any disruptive conduct. All spectators are advised to maintain silence throughout these proceedings . . . The defendant will approach the bench with counsel." Then to Robert Golub, ". . . You appear before the court under Indictment 71026 for sentence. Do the People wish to be heard?"

Cotter did. He spoke briefly to the court, making several points. "The bottom line, Judge, is that [Robert Golub] not only intended to kill [Kelly Tinyes], but he insured her death and he did it out of his own motivation to escape what he is about to receive here and that is the sentence for the acts that he committed against Kelly. I can't think of anything more brutal or savage. It is just beyond imagination that one human being can do this to another. . . ."

Cotter spoke of the impact this murder had on the

Tinyes family and on all of the children who lived on Horton Road. The probation report had indicated Robert's IQ was 132, ". . . and yet he chooses not to go to school. He chooses to take drugs and hang around the house . . . I don't know if he was born a murderer . . . I don't know how much is heredity and how much is environmental."

Cotter himself had received hundreds of letters and he summarized for the court what he thought they were all saying, the same sentiment he now wished to convey. "Please, Judge, protect us. Lock him up and throw away the key."

Marinello objected to comments he believed Cotter had made that were inflammatory. "Very frankly, Judge," he went on to say, "I can only indicate to you that during my representation of the defendant he has been cooperative to me. He has been intelligent, he understands the nature of this proceeding. He has been courteous and he has assisted in his defense . . . Normally I would be standing before this court indicating that this court should impose a less than maximum sentence and indicating what the mitigating circumstances are in his defense. However, I stand before the court indicating at the present time that since my representation of the defendant he has maintained his innocence throughout the proceedings. He has maintained his innocence at the time of arrest and he maintains his innocence today. . . ."

"Robert Golub," the judge said, "if there is anything you wish to say to this court before sentence is passed, you must do so now."

Robert addressed the court by reading from a prepared statement. "On the afternoon of March 4, 1989, a nightmare began for many people, including myself, my family and friends, the family and friends of the victim in this case and the many people who were involved in this investigation. . . ." In a hushed voice that was frequently inaudible to those in attendance, he hurried through his statement, claiming he had been sleeping when Kelly was murdered. After he was picked up by police, "I cooperated fully. I submitted fingerprints, hair samples, took a polygraph test, which I passed." In fact he had not passed, but the results of the test had not been placed in evidence during the trial and he could make the statement without contradiction.

"I did not kill Kelly Ann Tinyes," he said, as his voice quavered. "Who called Kelly up from upstairs from my home?" This was the first suggestion by anyone that Kelly had been called from an upstairs telephone in the Golubs' house. "Who let Kelly into our home . . . Who could have any motive? These are the questions I have to answer. These are the questions the jury should have considered. . . . If the real murderer is sitting here with us today, as sure as there is a God, it's not me." Wiping tears from his eyes, he continued, "I had many opportunities to run, should I have had reason . . . In all reality I was tried and convicted in the press with all the unfair portrayals, fingerpointing and malicious reporting. I never had a chance. . . ."

He went on to accuse the police of evidence tampering, the court of misconduct in refusing his request to have the trial moved and in dismissing his attorney, and finally the jury of impropriety. In his version of events he had been the victim of a massive conspiracy that encompassed every aspect of the investigation and analysis of the forensic evidence. The bloody latent print had been "a gross, misleading lie."

Yet so persuasive was he the chief clerk, who had witnessed many such speeches, questioned why he had not told his story to the jury. "For the first time I wondered" if he was guilty, the chief clerk acknowledged.

Now it was Judge Goodman's turn. "You, Robert Golub, who stand here today for sentencing in the most serious crime under the penal law of the State of New York, murder in the second degree, a jury of twelve citizens of this county, after over eight weeks of trial have found you guilty of intentional murder . . . You, Robert Golub, maintained your innocence and continue that through your own statement. That is your right, but the jury has decided otherwise and the evidence in this case shows otherwise. The acts which you committed in this case are by far the most atrocious that I have ever experienced in my seventeen years as a judge. And the manner in which you killed Kelly Ann Tinyes and mutilated her body surpasses the worst murders known to this county. No dictionary contains sufficient words to describe the brutality of your acts.

"Unfortunately, the sentence option given to me by our laws falls short of the sentence which you truly deserve. . . ." He urged any future parole board not to release Robert until he had served the maximum sentence. "You are hereby sentenced to a maximum term of life and to a minimum term of twenty-five years." This was the longest sentence New York law permitted.

When he finished there was no eruption in the courtroom when the words were spoken, or as Robert Golub was taken away in handcuffs.

In the hallway Richard Tinyes approached Wells. Throughout this exhausting process Tinyes had never once expressed a single word of appreciation for the job Wells and his men had done. Indeed, he had relentlessly criticized and second-guessed the investigation at nearly every opportunity. As Tinyes came up Wells anticipated the customary thanks the families of victims gave at such a moment. Instead Tinyes said, "Now maybe you'll get the other ones."

Twenty

The Tinyes family held a victory celebration at their house, which was brightly decorated with pink-and-white helium-filled balloons, then they granted still another interview to the press. Victoria, confident and outspoken, suggested the family may at last be satisfied "but there are a lot of unanswered questions." Richard was more direct. "I have strong feelings . . . that one person could not have done what they did to my daughter." He urged that the police investigation continue. Officers had commented more than once among themselves that Richard had come to enjoy his fifteen minutes of fame. Now he claimed for the first time that he had been threatened numerous times. "I didn't want anything to disturb the trial, so I didn't say anything," he said.

Down the street John Golub said he would consider moving if someone made a decent offer for his house, but he warned that if the harassment continued he would "become part of the war. If someone breaks my window, I will condone someone breaking their window."

In the months following the murder of her friend, Roberta Grosse had clipped every story about Kelly and carefully placed it into a scrapbook. It was a way of keeping her alive during that time. But as the trial came to an end, she could not bear to look at the scrapbook even when it was closed. She asked herself if this was how she wanted to remember Kelly. She finally threw the scrapbook into the garbage.

Her father was right. Nothing good will ever come out of Kelly's murder. "Here you have two families destroyed. You have a son in jail, and more than anything—Where's Kelly?"

Roberta had watched Robert's sentencing on television at home with her mother. Afterward she looked at her mother and asked, "Well, when does he get out?"

A few days later John Golub accepted $5,000 to appear on *A Current Affair*. The program would also air an interview with Robert Golub, and John said he had agreed to participate because the show was contributing the money toward his son's legal defense fund. Had the money gone directly to Robert it would have been illegal under New York state's then "Son of Sam" law, which prohibited criminals from profiting from their acts.

"I am outraged," Richard Tinyes said, "at the whole thought that the Golubs are trying to make money off of my daughter's brutal murder."

Robert told *A Current Affair* that he was confident his conviction would be reversed on appeal because "there were so many appealable issues. I don't really feel too much for myself. I feel for my family, the people who are worrying about me, who care about me."

As for the murder itself, "A very nice girl from my neighborhood is dead, bit I'm just not responsible. I'm doing everything I can to prove that I'm innocent. Hopefully the right person will be brought to justice. . . ."

"Kelly Ann was shockingly mutilated," the interviewer said. "Look me dead straight in the eye and tell me you had nothing to do with it."

"Oh, I'm certain I could," Robert answered.

"You totally deny any connection in the murder of young Kelly Ann Tinyes?"

"Oh, that's correct."

Asked his theory of the murder, "Well, my theory is it had to be somebody who knew her . . . I think it was a—I don't know—maybe an act of revenge . . ."

"Anyone who could do that to Kelly Ann," the interviewer said, "was a subhuman being."

"Oh, definitely," Robert agreed.

"How would you describe the kind of person who killed Kelly Ann?"

"Really, I don't think I've come in contact with the person who did this, or the likes of a person who did this in my entire lifetime . . . ," Robert replied, avoiding the question, saying later that the killer was "definitely not a sane human being." He insisted that the Golubs' house was "not a fortress, somebody can walk right in the front door." Still denying his guilt, he said, "I feel as strongly as anyone about the death of a young girl. Even if the Tinyes family believed in the worst way that I was the person that committed this crime" they should still leave his family in peace.

Richard Tinyes appeared by remote camera since he had refused to be in the same studio as the Golubs. The interviewer wanted to know "how decent people can behave indecently when you recognize that a little innocent girl was stolen from life."

Richard said, "You look into her room and it is empty. You don't hear her voice anymore. How do you say 'Happy Birthday' to her? You can't say 'Happy Birthday' to a tombstone."

Elizabeth Golub described the harassment to which she and her family had been subjected. She had lost forty pounds during the past year. She claimed she was at peace living in her home. "My nightmare is walking into and out of this house."

John Golub now spoke up. "I'll be dead when [my son] gets out. And when he is out what can I leave him? All of my money now goes to lawyer fees . . . What does he have when he gets out of jail at forty-five years old . . . ?"

The two lawyers had been interviewed as well. "Robert Golub is a psychopath," Cotter said. "He has a personality disorder that makes him an antisocial individual. He has a personality problem which is typical of someone who really has no conscience, he has no remorse for anything he does to somebody else."

Marinello saw it differently. "He is a very rational person. He is an intelligent person and, frankly speaking, if I were in his shoes and his position having been charged with this crime, I don't know if I could have maintained the same kind of presence and the same kind of rationality that he exhibited."

A Current Affair posted a rating of 11.4, up from the average 7.6. Local television stations also acknowledged higher ratings whenever they aired a report on the grisly murder and the ongoing fight between the families. *Newsday* didn't report the effect on its circulation.

Over thirty incidents of reported harassment occurred during the following weeks, with both sides asserting the other was the instigator. On September 11 Elizabeth Golub claimed that when she left for work that morning Victoria pulled alongside her car and screamed accusations at her that both she and her son were murderers. Instead of taking her usual route, Elizabeth turned to avoid a confrontation then drove down a residential street to reach work. She claimed Victoria drove her car directly at her from the opposite direction, changing lanes to do so. Elizabeth backed up out of the street and stopped to ask a woman pedestrian if she had seen what had just happened. A man ran up to her and said he had. Elizabeth filed a police report naming the witness. Victoria denied any knowledge of the incident, but because an independent witness corroborated what had taken place the police filed a charge of harassment, which carried a penalty of fifteen days in jail and a $250 fine.

Three weeks later Victoria was arraigned in another judicial circus as dozens of supporters appeared in support. A trial date was set and Victoria was admonished by the judge to "avoid any contact" with Elizabeth. In the hallway John Golub and Linda Player, standing with a group of supporters, exchanged accusations of "liar."

The prosecutor expressed his frustration at events. His office now had more than thirty-five complaints of incidents—at least twenty from the Golubs, fifteen from the Tinyes family. He was uncertain what to do and said he did not appreciate prosecuting the mother of a murder victim.

The case took a bizarre turn on October 3 when the trial was postponed amid allegations that the "independent" witness to the incident was, in fact, a friend of Robert's and a member of John Golub's yacht club.

All of the complaints to date were turned over to a grand jury for investigation.

Life on Horton Road had not returned to normal in the months following Robert's sentence. When Elizabeth Golub drove down the street, neighbors stopped what they were doing to stare. Supporters of the Tinyes family placed their hands on their hips and scowled. Elizabeth complained that Richie Tinyes mouthed obscenities at her; other children spit at her car as she drove by. One day young boys threw rocks at her as she washed her front window.

The Tinyes family had their complaints. Victoria claimed that Elizabeth yelled out to her one day that she belonged with her daughter. Richard said that John Golub persisted in his story that he had murdered Kelly.

A holiday did not pass that police officers weren't summoned by one, or both, of the families.

By late 1990 there were signs the neighborhood was growing weary of the combat. One neighbor who asked that her name not be used said the constant feuding was preventing the Tinyes family from grieving and that was not healthy—for them or the neighborhood. Another said the fighting was just causing more pain. As a rule the majority of the families were trying to stay out of it, but that wasn't always possible; and circumstances being what they were, it was impossible to sell a house and move away.

In December Elizabeth Golub's complaint was dropped as were all of the allegations of harassment before the grand jury. The Tinyes family had agreed to testify before it, but the Golubs refused cooperation unless granted immunity. "The charges were totally ridiculous," Richard Tinyes told reporters.

In April 1991 Nolan retired as a police officer and accepted a position as assistant vice president of the West Minster Bank. Richard Wells ended his twenty-seven-year career, taking medical retirement in September 1992, and spoke publicly for the first time. He said, "In my entire career, nothing compares to the absolute insanity of the Golub-Tinyes case. It's outrageous . . . This insanity has got to end before another tragedy happens." What he did not say was that the Tinyes murder investigation had nearly cost him his life, and in the end it cost him his career by damaging his health.

In retrospect the case against Robert appeared very strong, but at the time who had killed Kelly Ann Tinyes had been a mystery. Wells and the other detectives had spent weeks gathering microscopic bits of evidence and the case had been a triumph of the new science of DNA. Without the ability to match individual traces of blood to both Robert and Kelly, it was not likely there would have been an arrest. The expert testimony on the bite marks had created the last insurmountable barrier for the defense in its attempt to create a reasonable doubt, but it had been the DNA and its scientific certainty that had convicted Robert.

The aspect of the case which had given Wells his greatest pause had been the need to persuade the jury that the young clean-cut man was in reality a murderer. The crime had been so monstrous it defied reasoning.

There was one major, unresolved area which would now never be answered. Only after Robert had refused further questions did officers learn of his steroid use and abuse. Knowing what they did about how steroids contributed to anger and aggression, it appeared in retrospect that his use of the drug likely was a contributing factor in his loss of control and in the frenzy the day of the murder. Wells would never know for certain but the suspicion remained.

Another aspect of the case remained unresolved as well. Neither Wells nor Nolan was ever able to determine who on the investigative team had leaked information to the press.

In the end it had been Robert's steadfast commitment to his lies which had made his position untenable. Most criminals are undone because they tell someone. Robert had confessed to no one, but instead had been condemned by his lies. Had he said he discovered Kelly's body, believed John Jay murdered her, then concealed her in the closet, the conviction would have been much more difficult.

The condition of the Golubs' house and the feud between the families had diverted attention from the fact that the murder of Kelly Ann Tinyes had been a classic sexual-sadistic mutilation killing. Jack the Ripper had similarly disemboweled his victims. The beating, the strangling, the bites, the destruction of her sexual organs, were all signs of this type of well-established murder. It was not uncommon for such a killer to not have had sex with the victim, or to have attempted it with the dead body. Even Robert's sleeping so deeply in his room following the assault was straight out of a textbook.

Perpetrators of this type of crime held the impulse bottled for years struggling against the drives within them. They often found some release through drugs and alcohol. In Robert's case the loss of his job and the self-esteem that went with it, the idle hours alone in his house, made all the worse by the unavailability of his gym and the release he had received through his daily workouts, all led to that explosion.

Wells would never know how many times Robert had watched Kelly walking home, how often he had fantasized destroying her, how close he had come to acting before the day he finally did. When at last he had succumbed to the demons that raged in him, he had beaten, murdered, and mutilated her in a frenzy. Once he was sated the rudimentary mopping up after the murder would have taken every bit of discipline he could muster, and because the basement was so dirty bloodstains that would have been easily spotted in most homes passed unnoticed.

Then he had collapsed in his bed and very likely slept in a comatic state until awakened by his mother to have dinner. By then with the Tinyes family searching for their daughter, it was too late to dispose of the body.

Only the lingering hostility of Horton Road and Wells's premonition that another shoe had yet to drop robbed Wells of complete satisfaction at the case's outcome.

That summer the Tinyes family wrote New York governor Mario Cuomo in an attempt to persuade him to appoint a special prosecutor to reopen the case. They were convinced John Jay and other members of the family had participated in their daughter's murder. He declined, stating, "There was no basis for believing that the district attorney and the assistant district attorney were either unwilling or unable to do a thorough and complete job."

Allegations of harassment continued and there are today more than one hundred on file with the police by the families with dozens more from neighbors. Elizabeth Golub told friends that she periodically received calls on the telephone comprised of someone screaming, "Murderer! Murderer! Murderer!" On the street Victoria Tinyes would confront her and repeatedly shout, "You killed my daughter! You killed my daughter!'," as though the phrase had become a line in a catechism.

Richard Tinyes has stated that he will not move from Horton Road because he believes someday John Jay Golub will return and he must be there to protect the neighborhood from him.

Birdsall was promoted to detective and in July 1991 received the police department's Medal of Distinguished Service for his work in the case. He was given his choice of assignments and returned to regular investigative work. Ron Crowe was also promoted to detective. Ed Nawrocki retired. Whether the Golub murder investigation was the cause or not, he didn't say. Dan Cotter was appointed to the bench.

In May 1992 Elizabeth Golub reported to the police that Richie Tinyes, now eleven years old, threw leaves and grass at her in her car, then took a shopping cart and rammed it into the side of her car five times. He then placed the cart in front of her car so she could not drive off. When Elizabeth went to remove the cart, Victoria Tinyes confronted her and a shouting match erupted during which Victoria allegedly bumped into Elizabeth. When police responded Victoria was arrested for harassment. When she was scheduled to appear in court, the prosecutor offered to dismiss the charge. Victoria refused. The charge was dismissed that July.

In August John Golub was cited for allegedly ramming his car into the back of the pickup truck carrying Richard Tinyes and his son. Horton Road had been narrowed to a single one-way lane for repairs, and John claimed Richard intentionally stopped his car in front of him while a friend stopped in back to box John in. He acknowledged nudging the car out of place so he could pass. At his trial John Golub admitted throwing rocks at Victoria Tinyes and yelling an obscenity at her. He was acquitted of the charges after telling the jury he was afraid of the Tinyeses.

The following March Victoria sued the Golubs for $5 million dollars for false arrest.

In June 1993 John Golub claimed Victoria sprayed his passing car with her water hose. He stopped and exchanged words with her. Victoria alleged John had driven onto her lawn and tried to run her over. Both filed charges of harassment against the other; the cases were dismissed for lack of evidence.

Richie Tinyes now reports trouble sleeping at nights. John Jay Golub no longer lives in Valley Stream and at last report was using another name.

And life has been permanently altered for Roberta Grosse and Kelly's other friends as well. Murder is the most unkind way to lose a friend. For months after Kelly's death Roberta chastised herself when she laughed. How could she be happy when Kelly was dead?

And at first she thought of Kelly dozens of times a day. But when the trial began she thought about her less often and felt she was somehow betraying a friend. She came to realize, however, that what her mother said was right. Time does ease pain.

Roberta has grown up fast. From this experience she learned to take nothing in life for granted. It is, indeed, a brief candle. She lives not in fear of death, but with a love for life. And Kelly will "always be in my memories, and she's in everyone's heart."

The fight between the families now has a life of its own. Nolan calls it the "Holy War," though it is really no more than a sidebar in an otherwise precedent-setting homicide prosecution. The consequences of murder have brought out the worst in both families, and it is difficult to sympathize with either of them any longer. The Golubs are too stubborn to move; the Tinyeses too convinced of their own righteousness to walk away. It is as if almost anything is permissible in the name of Kelly's memory.

John Golub insists he believes his son is innocent, but in the three years following his conviction he only visited Robert in prison once, hardly the conduct of a man who truly believes his son wrongly imprisoned.

In the Tinyeses' house at 101 Horton Road, Kelly's room is untouched, left just as it was the last day of her life, a shrine in perpetuity. Every night Kelly's dog, Brutus, sleeps under her bed.

Four doors away at 81 Horton Road, Robert's room also remains undisturbed. Once a week Elizabeth Golub enters to water the plants. There is still no door.

For the Tinyeses and the Golubs time has stood still, frozen that terrible Saturday when officers discovered Kelly's body. The unnamed neighbor may well have been correct when she said the fight keeps the Tinyes family from grieving. Perhaps, on some level, that's what the conflict is really all about.

The feud might serve a similar purpose for the Golubs. As long as they remain on Horton Road and in defiance of the Tinyes family, they are victims themselves and must never face the reality of what their son had done.

Horton Road has been permanently altered. It has stopped being the neighborhood it once was and is unlikely ever to be again. "This was a great block," one neighbor observed. "It's been ruined."

And lying in Roberta Grosse's dresser is an unopened birthday gift. Inside is a pair of earrings for a thirteen-year-old girl, a present that will never be worn, a gift for a girl who no longer exists.

Kelly's friends are now young adults. What they have of her are a few photographs and dimming memories. They are moving on in their lives, to professions, to marriages, to joy, or to unhappiness. They will live their allotted years.

Kelly Ann Tinyes will remain always that thirteen-year-old girl on the eve of her fourteenth birthday.

And Robert Golub will be eligible for release when he is forty-six years old.

MORE MUST-READ TRUE CRIME
FROM PINNACLE

Under the Knife   0-7860-1197-1   **$6.50**US/**$8.50**CAN
By Karen Roebuck

Lobster Boy   0-7860-1569-1   **$6.50**US/**$8.50**CAN
By Fred Rosen

Body Dump   0-7860-1133-5   **$6.50**US/**$8.50**CAN
By Fred Rosen

Savage   0-7860-1409-1   **$6.50**US/**$8.50**CAN
By Robert Scott

Innocent Victims   0-7860-1273-0   **$6.50**US/**$8.50**CAN
By Brian J. Karem

The Boy Next Door   0-7860-1459-8   **$6.50**US/**$8.50**CAN
By Gretchen Brinck

Available Wherever Books Are Sold!

Visit our website at **www.kensingtonbooks.com**.

MORE MUST-READ TRUE CRIME
FROM PINNACLE

Feel the Seduction Of
Pinnacle Horror